The Four-Blocks® Literacy Model

Interactive Charts

Shared Reading for

Kindergarten and First Grade

by

Dorothy P. Hall
and
Karen L. Loman

Cover Design
Annette Hollister-Papp

Artists
Wayne Miller
Bill Neville
J. J. Rudisill

Editors
Joey Bland
Tracy Soles

Carson-Dellosa Publishing Company, Inc.
Greensboro, North Carolina

Table of Contents

See individual charts for corresponding take-home book pages.

Introduction

This book is about a special kind of shared or interactive reading and writing for kindergarten and early first grade called "interactive charts." Interactive charts provide young children the opportunity to manipulate text and interact with print as they learn to read the text. An interactive chart can be based on a nursery rhyme, a traditional or counting song, familiar poem or finger play, or any other theme or topic your class is studying. As emergent readers, young children are active, concrete learners who need a lot of support. Interactive charts can provide that support. Because these interactive charts are based on familiar and easy-to-learn rhymes, poems, and verses, young children learn to "say" the words quickly and then learn to "read" the words with a little more effort.

Interactive charts also help transfer oral language skills to written language skills. The charts help children begin to match oral words with written text and provide children with the opportunity to learn how to self-check and self-correct, or "cross-check." As children read these interactive charts, they gain control over printed words, and they develop an "I can read" attitude. This develops the "desire to read and write," one of the building blocks of success in kindergarten and early first grade.

Children who come to school reading, or ready to read, have had some reading and writing experiences that help them profit from school instruction. Some children, however, come to school lacking the skills and understanding that lead to success in beginning reading instruction. What can we do to help these children? Kindergarten and first-grade teachers can provide the necessary experiences for *all* of their students by:

- reading *to* children—both fiction and nonfiction.
- reading *with* children—shared reading of predictable books and interactive charts.
- providing opportunities for children to read *by themselves.*
- writing *for* children—a morning message at the start of each day.
- writing *with* children—predictable charts and interactive morning messages.
- providing opportunities for children to write *by themselves.*
- helping children develop phonemic awareness (the oral).
- emphasizing letters and sounds, or phonics (the written).
- helping children learn "interesting-to-them" words—names, environmental print, etc.

These activities are the basis of the Building Blocks™ program developed by Dorothy Hall and Patricia Cunningham. See *Month-by-Month Reading and Writing for Kindergarten* by Hall and Cunningham (Carson-Dellosa, 1997) and *The Teacher's Guide to Building Blocks™* by Hall and Williams (Carson-Dellosa, 2000) for detailed descriptions of this program.

Interactive charts are included in *The Teacher's Guide to Building Blocks™* (pages 84–88). Suggestions are given for making several interactive charts, such as a chart made from the traditional counting rhyme, "Five Little Monkeys."

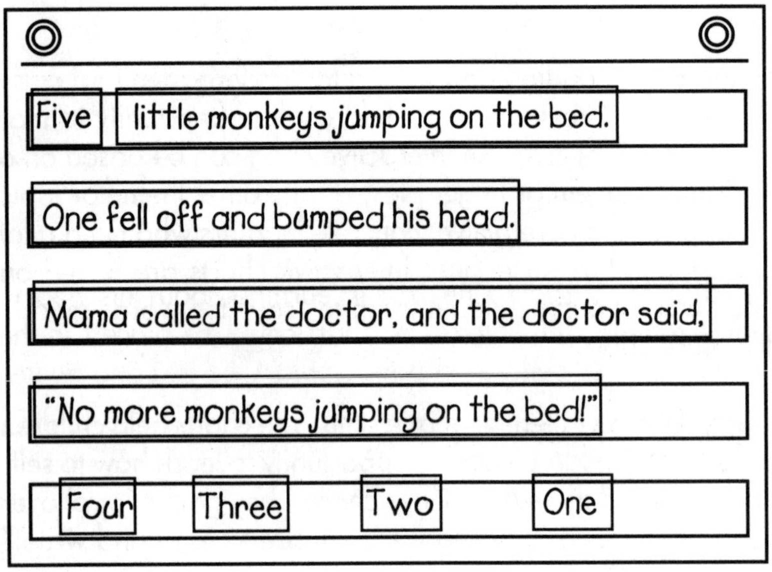

The first four lines are printed on sentence strips. The word that is manipulated in this text is the number word "five." The teacher makes four additional number word cards: four, three, two, and one. The children can manipulate the number word in the first sentence and read the chart five times. By using this interactive chart, the children can see that all the words are the same in each verse; only the number word changes. When the chart is put into a classroom reading center, the children can continue to "read" the chart, manipulate the words, and practice this new skill.

Another chart suggestion is a "Getting to Know You" chart, usually used at the beginning of the year with some get-acquainted activities to focus on a special child. The teacher writes four sentences on sentence strips and places them in a pocket chart. Each day, the teacher interviews the special student of the day and writes the four interactive portions.

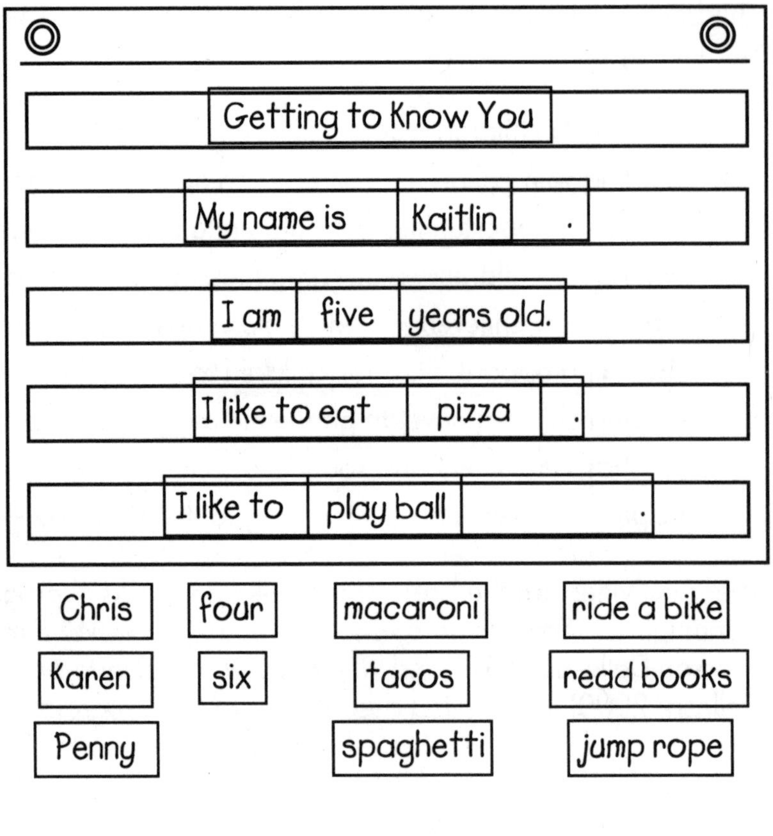

The first thing the teacher writes is the student of the day's name. She then places the student's name in the pocket chart to complete the first sentence. Next, the child tells how old he is, and the teacher writes the number word and places it in the pocket chart to complete the second sentence. Then, the student tells his favorite food to complete the third sentence. Finally, he tells a word or two about what he likes to do; this completes the final sentence. As the child dictates the words for each sentence, the teacher writes them down and then reads the sentences back to the class. This can be done in a pocket chart first and then rewritten on chart paper so that each child can illustrate his sentences. The finished charts can be displayed on a bulletin board or wall in the classroom. Young children are proud when they can read their own chart to family members and friends. Using the same four sentences over and over again helps all kindergarten and first-grade children accomplish this feat. The only word that is different on each chart is *their* name, *their* age, *their* favorite food, and what *they* like to do. Those are "important-to-them" words!

One other idea for interactive charts is to tie the chart to something the class is learning about in school—a theme. An interactive chart on "Plants" is an example. This interactive chart could be placed in the science center after using the chart with the whole class, so children can manipulate the text and review this science concept. Teachers can draw picture clues on the word cards to help emergent readers find the right word and cross-check the oral word with both the picture clue and the beginning letters in the text. This also helps students look at word length.

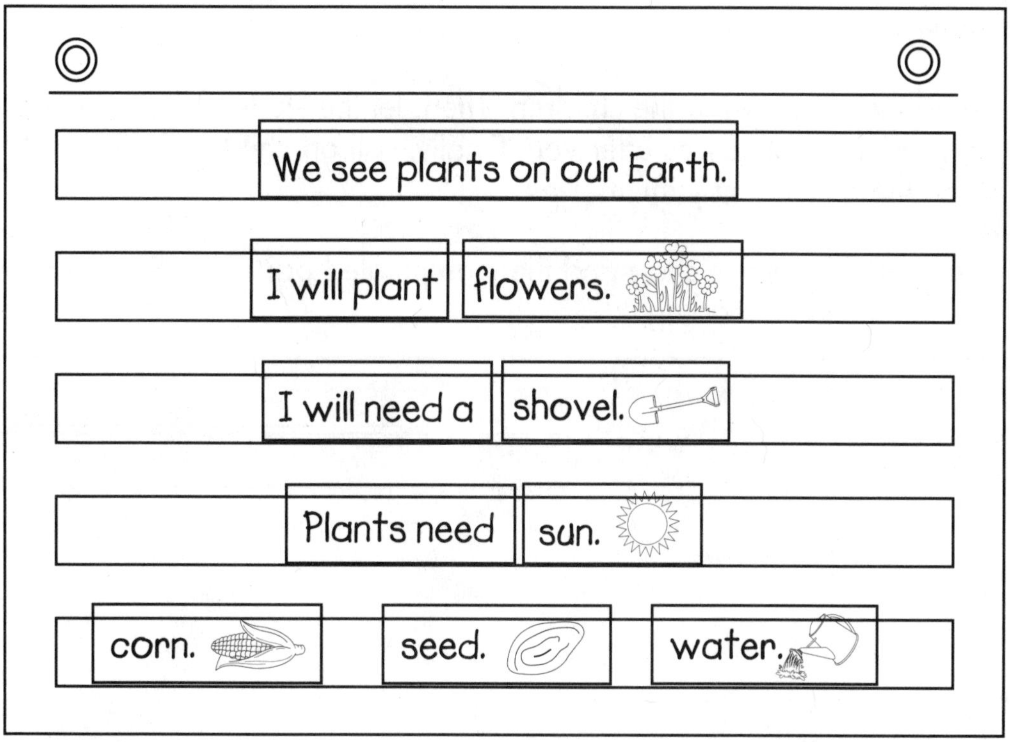

The steps for making an interactive chart are quite simple:

Steps for Making Interactive Charts

1. Write a song, poem, finger play, or verse on sentence strips, one sentence per strip. Or, write the sentences on lined chart paper. Four lines are appropriate for kindergarten or early first grade. Always use your best printing so that your students have a nice, neat model for handwriting. Be aware of the size, formation, and spacing of your writing.

2. Place the sentence strips in a pocket chart, or position the lined chart paper, where all the students can see it.

3. Choose a part of the sentence for the children to manipulate—a name, rhyming word, number word, etc., and make word cards using pieces of a sentence strip. When using sentence strips and a pocket chart, the manipulated part can be placed in the pocket chart at the correct spot. When using chart paper, the pieces of sentence strip can be attached to the chart with adhesive tape or hook-and-loop tape. You may also wish to place the chart on a magnetic white board and put magnetic tape on the back of the sentence strip pieces.

4. Read the sentences to the children. Then, let the students be your "echo" and read the sentences after you. Finally, call on children individually to read the sentences by themselves.

5. Place the interactive chart and the manipulated parts in a literacy center for independent reading.

How Interactive Charts Is a Multilevel Activity

Interactive charts, like interactive morning messages, are multilevel because we have different expectations for different children depending on their stage of literacy development. Some children will be able to read the entire chart, including all the words used for the interactive pieces. Other children will learn to read the number words, color words, or theme words that are repeated, or the repeated four lines on the chart. Still other children will be learning concepts of print as they do some shared reading after the initial echo reading led by the teacher. Children learn concepts of print as the teacher points to each of the words in each line of the text as she reads. This shows the children that we begin reading at the top left corner of a page and proceed to the right; then drop down a sentence, go back to the left, and read to the right with each new line. So, while some children are "really reading," other children are learning some new words, and still others are learning about print. Each child gets what she needs without being ability-grouped and having the teacher create three different lessons.

Using interactive charts can:

- increase exposure to print awareness.
- make songs, poems, and themes more meaningful to children.
- illustrate left-to-right print concept.
- illustrate top-to-bottom directionality.
- help students see words as units.
- encourage students to notice likenesses and differences between words.
- promote learning to read.
- help students see the natural flow of language.
- give students exposure to reading skills.
- promote individual reading success.
- develop word recognition skills.
- develop "tracking print" skills (one word/one touch awareness) through finger pointing.
- develop awareness that print conveys meaning.
- facilitate learning about letters and sounds.
- develop awareness of capital and lowercase letters.
- encourage students to contribute to class charts.
- give students an opportunity to understand what an interactive chart is and the idea that text can be manipulated.

Take-Home Books

Making small take-home books extends the interactive chart themes developed in the classroom. For example, the interactive chart on "Me," a common back-to-school theme, may be developed in the classroom. This interactive chart could be placed in the literacy center after introducing and practicing the chart with the whole class. In the literacy center, children can manipulate the text and review this important social studies concept by themselves and with their friends. Once children are familiar with the words and concepts in the chart, each child can make a take-home book so the learning can be extended to the home.

The process of making the books allows children to experience success as a reader and writer. Children will write and draw as much of the books on their own as is possible. Early books may need more assistance, but children will be able to make more and more of the books on their own as their reading and writing develop.

Reading their take-home books also helps students achieve some success. Each student should read the small books again and again at school and at home to themselves, friends, and family members. The rereading of a familiar text is one of the most valuable learning tools students can use to become accomplished readers.

Making a connection between home and school is another opportunity for students to achieve some success when they make take-home books. When children bring home books that contain the words and concepts introduced through interactive charts, parents can support the literacy skills developed at school. Parents can assist kindergarten and first-grade children by:

- reading the take-home books *to* their child.
- reading the take-home books *with* their child.
- providing opportunities for their child to read his take-home books *by himself.*

How to Use This Book

There are 48 ideas for interactive charts in this book, along with corresponding take-home book patterns. The charts are divided into sections: names, numbers, colors, animals, social studies, science, and a number of other themes.

Select a chart to make in the classroom, and then make it according to the directions given. Read the sentences from the chart to the children. Reread the chart several times using each of the manipulated text options. For example, the "Me" chart will have multiple choices for eye and hair color, student size, and smile description. Next, let the children be your "echo" and read the sentences after you. Finally, call on children to read the sentences by themselves. Place the chart and manipulated text in a literacy center for independent reading.

When the children are familiar with the chart and the manipulated text, have children make the corresponding take-home book. The student will "personalize" each take-home book by selecting one of the manipulative text options. For example, a "Me" take-home book might say:

My eyes are blue.

My hair is red.

My smile is big.

I am short.

I am just right!

Children should read their completed books to friends and teachers at school. Then, the books should be taken home and read to parents, grandparents, siblings, etc.

The take-home books are designed to be multilevel with varying amounts of provided support. Some take-home books are open-ended and students can write and draw whatever they want from the class chart. Some books are open-ended with specific pictures are provided for support. Some take-home books suggest the word students should write in their book so it matches the picture on the page. Other books have some print provided so students can read the words that match the pictures. The take-home books should be completed to either reflect personal information from each child or information that matches the pictures in the books. Use the following information as a guide to help students successfully complete the social studies and science take-home books.

Rainbows

Page 1 Each student should write the word for something in the classroom that might be red (apple, pencil box, tablet, etc.), then draw and color a picture to match.

Page 2 Each student should write the word for something in the classroom that might be orange (pumpkin, basket, chair, etc.), then draw and color a picture to match.

Page 3 Each student should write the word for something in the classroom that might be yellow (pencil, coat, desk, etc.), then draw and color a picture to match.

Page 4 Each student should write the word for something in the classroom that might be green (apple, chair, plant, etc.), then draw and color a picture to match.

Page 5 Each student should write the word for something in the classroom that might be blue (coat, pencil box, curtain, etc.), then draw and color a picture to match.

Page 6 Each student should write the word for something in the classroom that might be purple (notebook, tablet, chair, etc.), then draw and color a picture to match.

Post Office

Page 1 Each student should color the child to look like himself.

Page 2 Each student should write the name of someone (friend, mom, dad, grandmother, grandfather, etc.) to whom they would mail a letter and color the person to look like the recipient.

Page 3 Each student should write the name of the recipient, the appropriate pronoun, and the name of someone else to receive a postcard (this could say "you"). Each student should color the child to look like the second recipient.

Page 4 Each student should write name of the recipient and color the child to look like himself.

Page 5 Each student should color the child to look like the recipient.

Page 6 Each student should write his name on the line provided.

Travel

Page 1 Each student should color the children.

Page 2 Each student should write how she will travel (car, plane, van, etc.) and draw a picture illustrating that form of transportation.

Page 3 Each student should write where she will stay (motel, with grandma, in a motor home, etc.) and draw a picture of that place.

Page 4 Each student should write where she will go (museum, Florida, see grandma, etc.) and draw a picture of that place.

Page 5 Each student should color the family scene.

Page 6 Each student should write her name on the line provided.

Doctor's Office

Page 1 Each student should color the picture to look like himself and his doctor.

Page 2 Each student should write a word that describes his doctor (nice, smart, funny, etc.) and color the picture to look like his doctor.

Page 3 Each student should write a word for something his doctor might give him (sticker, medicine, prescription, etc.) and draw it in the doctor's hand.

Page 4 Each student should write what his doctor might tell him to do (take my medicine, drink juice, eat my vegetables, etc.) and any additional details he may want.

Page 5 Each student should color the picture to look like himself and his doctor.

Page 6 Each student should write his name on the line provided.

Grandparents' Day

Cover Each student should color the child and grandparents to look like her family.

Page 1 Each student should write a word that describes something she does with her grandfather and draw/color a picture of them doing that activity.

Page 2 Each student should write a word that describes something she does with her grandmother and draw/color a picture of them doing that activity.

Page 3 Each student should write a word that describes something she does with her grandparents and draw/color a picture of them doing that activity.

Page 4 Each student should write a word that describes a time she gets to see her grandparents (Thanksgiving, Christmas, birthdays, etc.) and color the picture.

Page 5 Each student should color the child and grandparents to look like her family.

Page 6 Each student should write her name on the line provided.

Bugs

Page 1 Each student should color the bugs to look like those he might see on the playground.

Page 2 Each student should choose words that tell the kind of bugs he might see on the playground (an ant, a spider, a beetle, etc.) and draw a picture of the bugs.

Page 3 Each student should write the name of the smallest bug of his three and draw the bug in the container.

Page 4 Each student should write the name of the largest bug of his three and draw the bug in the container.

Page 5 Each student should write the name of his favorite bug, why it is his favorite, and draw a picture of it.

Page 6 Each student should write his name on the line provided.

Birds

Page 1 Each student should color the picture and add any additional details to the picture she might need.

Page 2 Each student should write a word that tells something birds might have (wings, beaks, feathers, etc.), then draw and color a picture to match.

Page 3 Each student should write another word that tells something birds might have (wings, beaks, feathers, etc.), then draw and color a picture to match.

Page 4 Each student should write a word that describes birds (green, big, pretty, etc.) and add any additional details to the picture she might need.

Page 5 Each student should write a word that tells something birds might eat (seeds, berries, worms, etc.), then draw and color a picture to match.

Page 6 Each student should write her name on the line provided.

Pets

Page 1 Each student should color the picture and add any additional details to the picture he might need.

Page 2 Each student should add any additional details to the picture he might need, then color the picture.

Page 3 Each student should write a word or phrase that describes something dogs do (bark, run, play, etc.), then color the picture.

Page 4 Each student should add any additional details to the picture he might need, then color the picture.

Page 5 Each student should write a word or phrase that describes something cats do (purr, scratch, sleep, etc.), then color the picture.

Page 6 Each student should color the picture and add any additional details to the picture he might need.

Page 7 Each student should write a word or phrase that describes something fish do (swim, jump, dive, etc.), then color the picture.

Winter

Page 1 Each student should color the picture.

Page 2 Each student should write a word that tells something that might happen in the winter (snows, gets cold, etc.), then color the picture.

Page 3 Each student should write a word that tells something people might wear in the winter (coats, hats, gloves, etc.), then color the picture.

Page 4 Each student should write a word that tells something they might make in the winter (snowman, snowball, snow fort, etc.), then color the picture.

Page 5 Each student should color the picture.

Page 6 Each student should write her name on the line provided.

Spring

Page 1 Each student should color the picture.

Page 2 Each student should write a word that tells something that happens in spring (it rains, we see rainbows, gets warm, etc.), then color the picture.

Page 3 Each student should write a word that tells something people might wear in the spring (raincoats, jackets, rain boots, etc.), then color the picture.

Page 4 Each student should write a word that tells something he might plant in the spring (flowers, trees, grass, etc.), then color the picture.

Page 5 Each student should color the picture.

Page 6 Each student should write his name on the line provided.

Summer

Page 1 Each student should color the picture.

Page 2 Each student should write a word that describes summer (hot, dry, sunny, etc.), then color the picture.

Page 3 Each student should write a word that tells something she might do in the summer (swim, play, swing, etc.), then color the picture.

Page 4 Each student should write a word that tells how or what she might play in the summer (all day, baseball, tag, etc.), then color the picture.

Page 5 Each student should write a word that tells why summer is special (take vacations, see my grandma, play outside, etc.), then color the picture.

Page 6 Each student should write her name on the line provided.

Fall

Page 1 Each student should color the picture.

Page 2 Each student should write a word that describes what happens to leaves in the fall (change, turn colors, die, etc.), then color the picture.

Page 3 Each student should write a word that describes what happens to leaves in the fall (fall, are orange, etc.), then color the picture.

Page 4 Each student should write a word or phrase that tells something he might do in the fall (go back to school, play football, trick-or-treating, etc.), then color the picture.

Page 5 Each student should color the picture.

Page 6 Each student should write his name on the line provided.

Sun and Moon

Page 1 Each student should color the sun and moon and add any additional details to the picture.

Page 2 Each student should write a word that describes the sun (hot, big, yellow, etc.), then color the picture.

Page 3 Each student should tell what the sun provides (light, heat, warmth, etc.), then color the picture.

Page 4 Each student should write a word that describes the moon (big, white, far away, etc.), then color the picture.

Page 5 Each student should tell what the moon does (shines, changes shape, comes out at night, etc.), then color the picture.

Page 6 Each student should write his name on the line provided.

The Sky

Page 1 Each student should color the picture and any additional details she wants.

Page 2 Each student should describe the sky (clear, cloudy, blue, gray, etc.), then color the picture to match.

Page 3 Each student should describe something that falls from the sky (snow, sleet, rain, etc.), then color the picture.

Page 4 Each student should describe something that flies through the sky (birds, planes, butterflies, etc.), then color the picture to match.

Page 5 Each student should color the picture to look like herself.

Page 6 Each student should write her name on the line provided.

Plants

Page 1 Each student should color the plants.

Page 2 Each student should write word that describes something he might plant (seeds, flowers, pumpkins, etc.), then add any additional details to the picture.

Page 3 Each student should write a word that describes something he needs to plant (shovel, hoe, dirt, etc.), then add any additional details to the picture.

Page 4 Each student should write a word that describes something plants need (sun, warmth, heat, etc.), then color the picture.

Page 5 Each student should write a word that describes something plants need (water, rain, moisture, etc.), then color the picture.

Water

Page 1 Each student should color the picture and add any additional details to the picture.

Page 2 Each student should describe where water can be found (rivers, lakes, ponds, etc.), then add additional sources of water to the picture.

Page 3 Each student should color the picture, then add details to the picture

Page 4 Each student should write words that tell how people use water (drink, wash dishes, brush our teeth, etc.), then add details to the picture.

Page 5 Each student should write words that tell how people use water (wash our hands, keep clean, brush our teeth, etc.), then add details to the picture.

Page 6 Each student should color the picture.

Transportation

Page 1 Each student should add details, then color the picture.

Page 2 Each student should add details, then color the picture.

Page 3 Each student should add details, then color the picture.

Page 4 Each student should add details, then color the picture.

Page 5 Each student should add details, then color the picture.

Page 6 Each student should add details, then color the picture.

Page 7 Each student should add details, then color the picture.

Page 8 Each student should add details, then color the picture.

Page 9 Each student should add details, then color the picture.

Page 10 Each student should add details, then color the picture.

Page 11 Each student should write one kind of transportation that she has used on the line, then draw a picture of it in the space provided.

Page 12 Each student should write her favorite transportation on the line, then draw a picture of it in the space provided.

Page 13 Each student should write one kind of transportation that she wants to use on the line, then draw a picture of it in the space provided.

Page 14 Each student should write her name on the line provided.

Steps for Assembling the Take-Home Books:

Step 1. Select a take-home book for the class to make and remove the page(s) from this book.

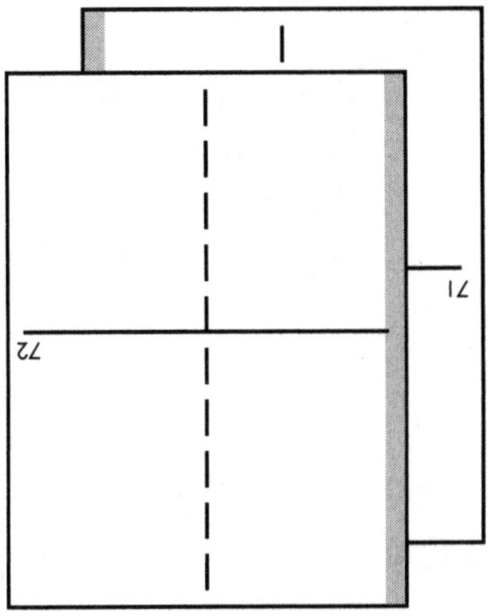

Step 2. Place the book page on the copier with the perforated edge on the right. Copy that side, then flip the page so that the perforated edge is still on the right. Copy that side of the page. Then, make a duplex (double-sided copy) of the new take-home book pages. (Be sure to place the pages so the page number for the top page is on the left and the page number for the bottom page is on the right.) Repeat this step for each page of the selected take-home book.

Step 3. Make enough double-sided copies of the copied take-home book page(s) for each child in the class.

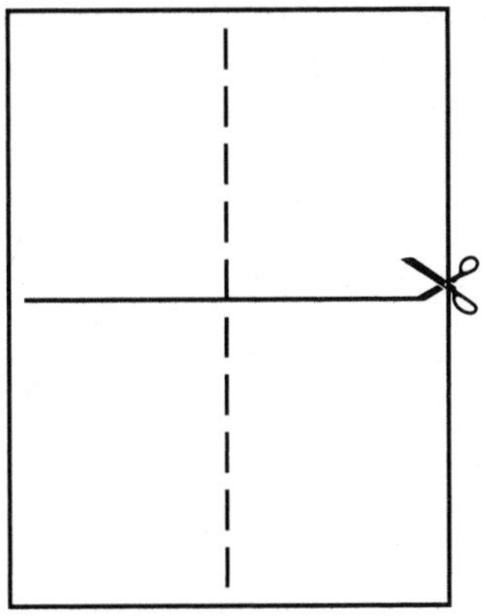

Step 4. Cut each page in half on the solid line.

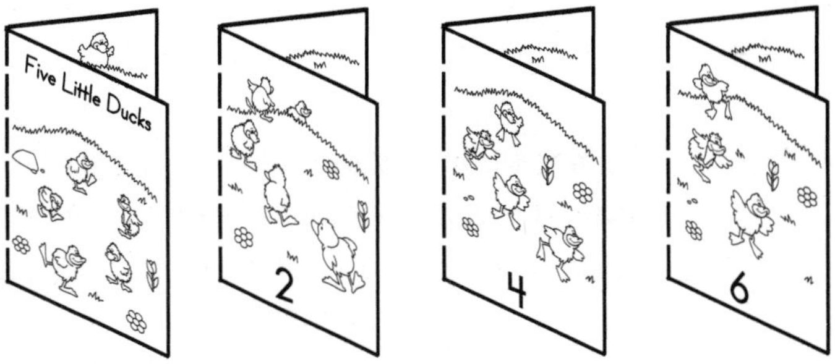

Step 5. Then, fold each 1/2 page along the dashed line and arrange the pages in order, placing the page with the cover on the outside.

Step 6. Staple the folded edge to keep the book together.

Step 7. Each student may then complete the pages by writing and drawing on them.

Jack Be Nimble

Preparation:
Make the "Jack Be Nimble" chart using either lined chart paper or sentence strips and a pocket chart. Write each child's name on three word cards or pieces of sentence strips.

Jack Be Nimble

Jack be nimble,
Jack be quick.
Jack jump over the candlestick.

Steps:

1. Introduce the interactive chart to students during "big group" time.
2. Read the original rhyme to the class several times.
3. Model how to cover the name in the rhyme with another student's name cards. For example, show how the name "Jack" can be replaced with Erica's name cards. Then, read the new rhyme to and with the class.

   Erica be nimble,
   Erica be quick.
   Erica jump over the candlestick.
4. Repeat with additional names until the children can easily read the rhyme.
5. Place the interactive chart in the reading center, along with the students' name cards. You may want to place each child's cards in a small, resealable bag and label the bag with the child's name.
6. During center time, the children can choose their name or a friend's name and complete the interactive chart. Once a student has completed the chart, have him read the chart to another student in the center.
7. Give each child a copy of the "Jack Be Nimble" take-home book (see pattern on pages 65-66) and let him illustrate it. For this take-home book, have the children write a different name on pages 4, 5, and 6.
8. Once a student completes his take-home book, have him read the book to a classmate.
9. Send the take-home books home with the students, and have students read the books to their parents, grandparents, siblings, etc.

Rain

Preparation:
Make the "Rain" chart using either lined chart paper or sentence strips and a pocket chart. Write each child's name on a word card or piece of sentence strip.

Rain

Rain, rain, go away,
Come again another day;
Little Johnny wants to play.

Steps:

1. Introduce the interactive chart to students during "big group" time.
2. Read the original rhyme to the class several times.
3. Model how to cover the name in the rhyme with another student's name card. For example, show how the name "Johnny" can be replaced with Hannah's name card. Then, read the new rhyme to and with the class.

   Rain, rain, go away,
   Come again another day;
   Little Hannah wants to play.
4. Repeat with additional names until the children can easily read the rhyme.
5. Place the interactive chart in the reading center, along with the students' word cards. You may want to place each card in a small, resealable bag and label the bag with the child's name.
6. During center time, the children can choose their names or a friend's name and complete the interactive chart. Once a student has completed the chart, have her read the chart to another student in the center.
7. Give each child a copy of the "Rain" take-home book (see pattern on pages 67-68) and let her illustrate it. For this take-home book, have the children write a different name on page 6.
8. Once a student completes her take-home book, have her read the book to a classmate.
9. Send the take-home books home with the students, and have students read the books to their parents, grandparents, siblings, etc.

Cookie Jar

Preparation:
Make the "Cookie Jar" chart using either lined chart paper or sentence strips and a pocket chart. Write each child's name on a word card or piece of sentence strip.

Cookie Jar
Who stole the cookie from the cookie jar?
Howard stole the cookie from the cookie jar.
Who, me?
Yes, you!
Not I.
Then, who?

Steps:

1. Introduce the interactive chart to students during "big group" time.
2. Read the original rhyme to the class several times.
3. Model how to cover the name in the rhyme with another student's name card. For example, show how the name "Howard" can be replaced with Linda's name card. Then, read the new rhyme to and with the class.

   Who stole the cookie from the cookie jar?
   Linda stole the cookie from the cookie jar.
   Who, me?
   Yes, you!
   Not I.
   Then, who?

4. Repeat with additional names until the children can easily read the rhyme.
5. Place the interactive chart in the reading center, along with the students' name cards. You may want to place each card in a small, resealable bag and label the bag with the child's name.
6. During center time, the children can choose their name or a friend's name and complete the interactive chart. Once a student has completed the chart, have him read the chart to another student in the center.
7. Give each child a copy of the "Cookie Jar" take-home book (see pattern on pages 69-70) and let him illustrate it.
8. Once a student completes his take-home book, have him read the book to a classmate.
9. Send the take-home books home with the students, and have students read the books to their parents, grandparents, siblings, etc.

Polly and Sukey

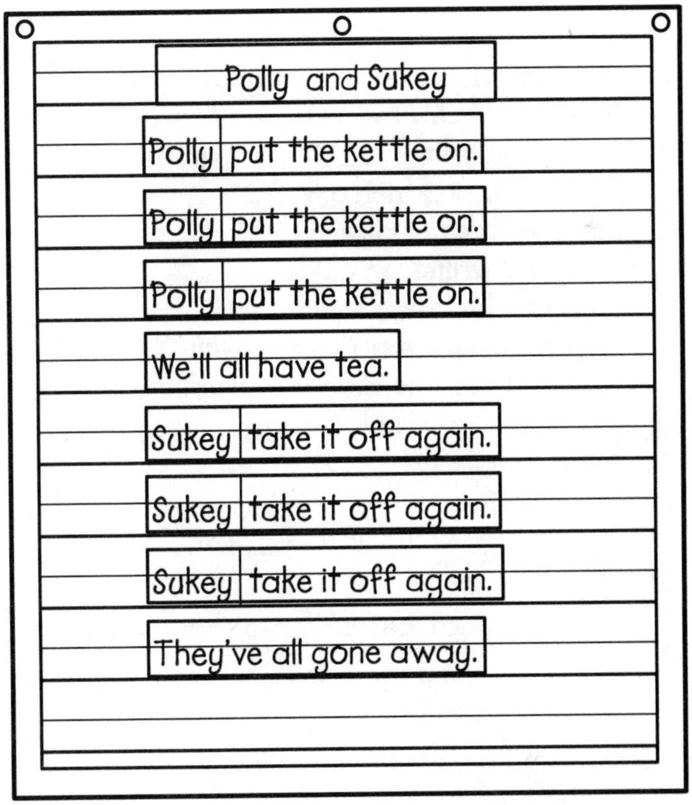

Preparation:
Make the "Polly and Sukey" chart using either lined chart paper or sentence strips and a pocket chart. Write each child's name on three word cards or pieces of sentence strips.

Steps:

1. Introduce the interactive chart to students during "big group" time.
2. Read the original rhyme to the class several times.
3. Model how to cover the names in the rhyme with two other students' name cards. For example, show how the name "Polly" can be replaced with Rene's name card, and "Sukey" can be replaced with Jason's name card. Then, read the new rhyme to and with the class.

   Rene, put the kettle on.
   Rene, put the kettle on.
   Rene, put the kettle on.
   We'll all have tea.

   Jason, take it off again.
   Jason, take it off again.
   Jason, take it off again.
   They've all gone away.

4. Repeat with additional names until the children can easily read the rhyme.
5. Place the interactive chart in the reading center, along with the students' name cards. You may want to place each card in a small, resealable bag and label the bag with the child's name.
6. During center time, the children can choose their name or a friend's name and complete the interactive chart. Once a student has completed the chart, have her read the chart to another student in the center.
7. Give each child a copy of the "Polly and Sukey" take-home book (see pattern on pages 71-72) and let her illustrate it.
8. Once a student completes her take-home book, have her read the book to a classmate.
9. Send the take-home books home with the students, and have students read the books to their parents, grandparents, siblings, etc.

A, My Name Is . . .

Preparation:
Make the "A, My Name Is . . ." chart using either lined chart paper or sentence strips and a pocket chart. Words are chosen for each letter and written on cards. This chart can be used to review letter sounds at the end of the year with your students. The chart uses cards for letters, names, places, and things people sell.

A, My Name Is . . .

A, my name is Akeesha.
My husband's name is Arnold.
We come from Alabama.
And we sell apples.

Steps:

1. Introduce the interactive chart to students during "big group" time.
2. Read the original rhyme to the children several times.
3. Model how to cover the "letter" in the rhyme with another letter and then find a girl's name and a boy's name to fill in the missing parts in the first and second lines.

   Find a "place" for the third line and a "product" for the fourth line. (You can use pictures to help with what the people sell.) Then, read the new rhyme to and with the class.

   Read the new rhyme(s). For example:

   B, my name is Betty.
   My husband's name is Bobby.
   We come from Boston.
   And we sell balloons.
4. Repeat with other letters and names until the children can easily read the rhyme. Have fun!
5. Place the interactive chart in the reading center, along with the word cards for each letter. You may want to place the cards for each letter in a small, resealable bag and label the bag with the letter.
6. Give each child a copy of the "A, My Name Is . . ." take-home book (see pattern on pages 73-74) and let him illustrate it.
7. Once a student completes his take-home book, have him read the book to a classmate.
8. Send the take-home books home with the students, and have students read the books to their parents, grandparents, siblings, etc.

Five Little Ducks

Preparation:
Make the "Five Little Ducks" chart using either lined or chart paper or sentence strips and a pocket chart. Write each number word, from "One" to "Four," on word cards or pieces of sentence strips.

Five Little Ducks
Five little ducks went out to play.
Over the hills and far away.
Mama Duck said, "Quack, quack, quack."
Four little ducks came running back.

Steps:

1. Introduce the interactive chart to students during "big group" time.
2. Read the original rhyme to the class several times.
3. Model how to cover each number in the rhyme with a different number. For example, show how "Five" can be replaced with "Four," and "Four" can be replaced by "Three." Then, read the new rhyme to and with the class.

   Four little ducks went out to play,
   Over the hills and far away.
   Mama Duck said, "Quack, quack, quack."
   Three little ducks came running back.
4. Repeat with additional numbers until the children can easily read the rhyme.
5. Place the interactive chart in the reading center, along with the number cards.
6. During center time, have children work with partners to change the number words and read the chart. You may want to have a pointer at the center, so one child can be the "teacher" as he works with the other student.
7. Give each child a copy of the "Five Little Ducks" take-home book (see pattern on pages 75-78) and let her illustrate it.
8. Once a student completes her take-home book, have her read the book to a classmate.
9. Send the take-home books home with the students, and have students read the books to their parents, grandparents, siblings, etc.

Six in the Bed

Preparation:
Make the "Six in the Bed" chart using either lined chart paper or sentence strips and a pocket chart. Write each number word, from one to five, on word cards or pieces of sentence strips.

Six in the Bed
There were six in the bed
And the little one said,
"Roll over. Roll over."
So they all rolled over
And one fell out.

Steps:

1. Introduce the interactive chart to students during "big group" time.
2. Read the original rhyme to the class several times.
3. Model how to cover the number in the rhyme with a different number. For example, show how "six" can be replaced with "five." Then, read the new rhyme to and with the class.

   There were five in the bed
   And the little one said,
   "Roll over. Roll over."
   So they all rolled over
   And one fell out.
4. Repeat with additional numbers until the children can easily read the rhyme.
5. Place the interactive chart in the reading center, along with the number cards. (You may want to make additional number cards from numbers seven to ten as the children learn them.)
6. During center time, have children work with partners to change the number words and read the chart. You may want to have a pointer at the center, so one child can be the "teacher" as she works with the other student.
7. Give each child a copy of the "Six in the Bed" take-home book (see pattern on pages 79-84) and let him illustrate it. Students should draw the number of children in the bed to match the text on each page.
8. Once a student completes his take-home book, have him read the book to a classmate.
9. Send the take-home books home with the students, and have students read the books to their parents, grandparents, siblings, etc.

Five Green Bottles

Preparation:
Make the "Five Green Bottles" chart using either lined chart paper or sentence strips and a pocket chart. Write each number word, from one to four, on three cards. For example, the number *four* cards would be Four, Four, and four. Write *no* on one card.

Five Green Bottles
Five green bottles sitting on the wall,
Five green bottles sitting on the wall,
And if one green bottle should accidentally fall,
There'd be four green bottles sitting on the wall.

Steps:

1. Introduce the interactive chart to students during "big group" time.
2. Read the original rhyme to the class several times.
3. Model how to cover the numbers in the rhyme with other number cards. For example, show how "Five" can be replaced with "Four," and "four" can be replaced with "three." Then, read the new rhyme to and with the class.

   Four green bottles sitting on the wall,
   Four green bottles sitting on the wall,
   And if one green bottle should accidentally fall,
   There'd be three green bottles sitting on the wall.
4. Repeat with additional numbers until the children can easily read the rhyme.
5. Place the interactive chart in the reading center, along with the number cards.
6. During center time, have children work with partners to change the number words and read the chart. You may want to have a pointer at the center, so one child can be the "teacher" as he works with the other student.

   You can also change the color word and/or the item (any two-syllable word) hanging on the wall.

   Five blue pictures . . .
   Five red ribbons . . .
   Five yellow paintings . . .
7. Give each child a copy of the "Five Green Bottles" take-home book (see pattern on pages 85-88) and let her illustrate it.
8. Once a student completes her take-home book, have her read the book to a classmate.
9. Send the take-home books home with the students, and have students read the books to their parents, grandparents, siblings, etc.

This Old Man

Preparation:
Make the "This Old Man" chart using either lined chart paper or sentence strips and a pocket chart. Write each number word, from one to ten, on word cards or pieces of sentence strips.

This Old Man
This old man,
He played one,
He played knick knack with his thumb.
With a knick knack, paddy whack,
Give a dog a bone,
This old man came rolling home.

Also write the rhyming phrase for each number ("on my shoe" for the number two) on a word card or piece of sentence strip.

two – on my shoe	five – on a hive	eight – on a gate
three – on my knee	six – with his sticks	nine – on my spine
four – at my door	seven – with his pen	ten – in my den

Steps:

1. Introduce the interactive chart to students during "big group" time.
2. Read the original rhyme to the class several times.
3. Model how to cover the number word and the rhyming phrase with another number word and rhyming phrase. For example, show how "one" can be replaced with "two" and the words "with his thumb" can be replaced with "on my shoe." Then, read the new rhyme to and with the class.

   This old man,
   He played two,
   He played knick knack on my shoe.
   With a knick knack, paddy whack,
   Give a dog a bone,
   This old man came rolling home.
4. Repeat with additional numbers and rhyming phrases until the children can easily read the rhyme.
5. Place the interactive chart in the reading center, along with the number and rhyming phrase cards. You may want to place each number card and its corresponding rhyming phrase in a small, resealable plastic bag and label the bag with the number.
6. Give each child a copy of the "This Old Man" take-home book (see pattern on pages 89-92) and let him illustrate it.
7. Once a student completes his take-home book, have him read the book to a classmate.
8. Send the take-home books home with the students, and have students read the books to their parents, grandparents, siblings, etc.

The Flowerpot

Preparation:
Make a the "The Flowerpot" chart using either lined chart paper or sentence strips and a pocket chart. Write several color words on cards or pieces of sentence strips using colorful markers to match the color words.

The Flowerpot
Pretty little flower
In a yellow pot.
Put it on the table.
What a nice spot!

Steps:

1. Introduce the interactive chart to students during "big group" time.
2. Read the original rhyme to the class several times.
3. Model how to cover the color word in the rhyme with another color word. For example, show how "yellow" can be replaced with "blue." Then, read the new rhyme to and with the class.

   Pretty little flower
   In a blue pot.
   Put it on the table.
   What a nice spot!
4. Repeat with additional color words until the children can easily read the rhyme.
5. Place the interactive chart in the reading center, along with the color cards.
6. During center time, the children can choose color cards to complete the interactive chart. Once a student has completed the chart, have him read the chart to another student in the center.
7. Give each child a copy of the "The Flowerpot" take-home book (see pattern on pages 93-94) and let him illustrate it.
8. Once a student completes his take-home book, have him read the book to a classmate.
9. Send the take-home books home with the students, and have students read the books to their parents, grandparents, siblings, etc.

Mary Wore a Red Dress

Preparation:
Make the "Mary Wore a Red Dress" chart using either lined chart paper or sentence strips and a pocket chart. Write each child's name on two cards or pieces of sentence strips. Write several color words on four cards using markers to match the color words.

Mary Wore a Red Dress
Mary wore a red dress, red dress, red dress.
Mary wore a red dress all day long.

Also prepare four word cards for each clothing item, but wait until the children suggest the items before writing them down.

Steps:

1. Introduce the interactive chart to stud ents during "big group" time.
2. Read the original rhyme to the class several times.
3. Tell the children you are going to use their names in the rhyme. Ask them to help you think of color words (blue, pink, orange, purple, green, yellow, etc.) and clothing items (jeans, sweater, vest, pants, sneakers, shirt, etc.).
4. Complete any word cards that are not yet written.
5. Model how to cover the name, color, and clothing cards in the rhyme with other cards. For example, show how "Mary" can be replaced with "Sidney," "red" can be replaced with "blue," and "dress" can be replaced with "jeans." Then, read the new rhyme to and with the class.

   Sidney wore blue jeans, blue jeans, blue jeans.
   Sidney wore blue jeans all day long.
6. Repeat the rhyme using several other children's names, color words, and clothing items until the children can easily read the rhyme.
7. Place the interactive chart in the reading center, along with the name, color, and clothing cards. You may want to sort the cards in small, resealable plastic bags labeled by name, color, and clothing.
8. During center time, have children work with partners to change the name, color, and clothing words and read the chart. You may want to have a pointer at the center, so one child can be the "teacher" as she works with the other student.
9. Give each child a copy of the "Mary Wore a Red Dress" take-home book (see pattern on pages 95-96) and let her illustrate it.
10. Once a student completes her take-home book, have her read the book to a classmate.
11. Send the take-home books home with the students, and have students read the books to their parents, grandparents, siblings, etc.

What Is It?

Preparation:
Make the "What Is It?" chart using either lined chart paper or sentence strips and a pocket chart. Write several color words on cards or pieces of sentence strips using colorful markers to match the color words.

What Is It?
Shiny green wings
With a little yellow spot.
Fuzzy brown body.
A caterpillar it's not.
What is it?

Steps:

1. Introduce the interactive chart to students during "big group" time.
2. Read the original rhyme to the class several times.
3. Model how to cover the color words in the rhyme with other color words. For example, show how "green" can be replaced with "yellow," "yellow" can be replaced with "red," and "brown" can be replaced with "orange." Then, read the new rhyme to and with the class.

   Shiny yellow wings
   With a little red spot.
   Fuzzy orange body,
   A caterpillar it's not.
   What is it?

4. Repeat the rhyme using several other color words until the children can easily read the rhyme.
5. Place the interactive chart in the reading center, along with the color cards.
6. During center time, the children can choose their favorite colors to complete the interactive chart. Once a student has completed the chart, have him read the chart to another student in the center.
7. Give each child a copy of the "What Is It?" take-home book (see pattern on pages 97-98) and let him illustrate it.
8. Once a student completes his take-home book, have him read the book to a classmate.
9. Send the take-home books home with the students, and have students read the books to their parents, grandparents, siblings, etc.

Crayons

Preparation:
Make the "Crayons" chart using either lined chart paper or sentence strips and a pocket chart. Write several color words on cards or pieces of sentence strips using colorful markers to match the color word.

Crayons
First use the blue,
Then, the red one.
Put them all away
When you are done.

Steps:

1. Introduce the interactive chart to students during "big group" time.
2. Read the original rhyme to the class several times.
3. Model how to cover the color words in the rhyme with other color words. For example, show how "blue" can be replaced with "yellow" and "red" can be replaced with "brown." Then, read the new rhyme to and with the class.

   First use the yellow,
   Then, the brown one.
   Put them all away
   When you are done.
4. Repeat the rhyme using several other color words until the children can easily read the rhyme.
5. Place the interactive chart in the reading center, along with the color cards.
6. During center time, the children can choose their favorite colors to complete the interactive chart. Once a student has completed the chart, have her read the chart to another student in the center.
7. Give each child a copy of the "Crayons" take-home book (see pattern on pages 99-100) and let her illustrate it.
8. Once a student completes her take-home book, have her read the book to a classmate.
9. Send the take-home books home with the students, and have students read the books to their parents, grandparents, siblings, etc.

Note: Due to the number of cards that must be created, this is a two-day activity.

Teddy Bear, Teddy Bear

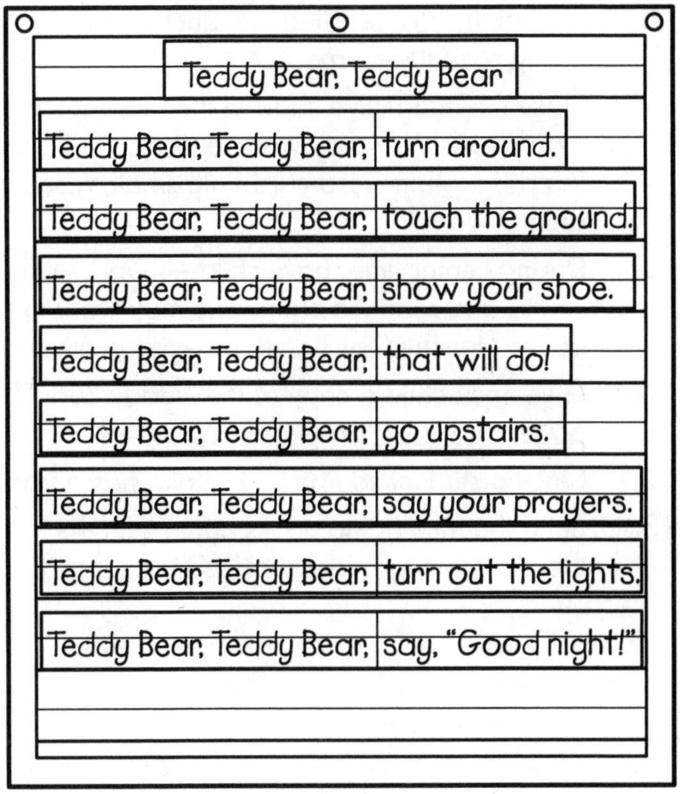

Teddy Bear, Teddy Bear
Teddy Bear, Teddy Bear, turn around.
Teddy Bear, Teddy Bear, touch the ground.
Teddy Bear, Teddy Bear, show your shoe.
Teddy Bear, Teddy Bear, that will do!
Teddy Bear, Teddy Bear, go upstairs.
Teddy Bear, Teddy Bear, say your prayers.
Teddy Bear, Teddy Bear, turn out the lights.
Teddy Bear, Teddy Bear, say, "Good night!"

Preparation:
Make the "Teddy Bear, Teddy Bear" chart using sentence strips in a pocket chart.* Write "Teddy Bear, Teddy Bear" on one strip and the action on another. Prepare eight sentence strips for each line change but wait for the children to make suggestions before writing.

Steps:

1. Introduce the interactive chart to students during "big group" time.
2. Read the original rhyme to the class several times. Explain to children that this is a jumping rope rhyme.(At an appropriate time, practice the rhyme with children while they are jumping rope.)
3. Ask the children to help you think of other animals that would fit in the rhyme (dog, cat, mouse, pig, bird, etc.). Write these on the board with a space in front of them for the describing word.
4. Then, ask the students to think of words that describe what that animal might look like (yellow, furry, little, pink, pretty). Write these on the board in the spaces in front of the animal words.
5. At a later time, complete the word cards, eight for each describing word and corresponding animal word (Yellow Dog, Furry Cat, Little Mouse, Pink Pig, Pretty Bird, etc.).
6. Share the chart at "big group" time on the following day.
7. Model how to replace the animal and describing words with different animal and describing words to make a new rhyme. For example, show how to replace "Teddy Bear" with "Yellow Dog" in the pocket chart. Then, read the new rhyme to and with the class.

   Yellow Dog, Yellow Dog, turn around.
   Yellow Dog, Yellow Dog, touch the ground.
   Yellow Dog, Yellow Dog, show your shoe.
   Yellow Dog, Yellow Dog, that will do!
   Yellow Dog, Yellow Dog, go upstairs.
   Yellow Dog, Yellow Dog, say your prayers.
   Yellow Dog, Yellow Dog, turn out the lights.
   Yellow Dog, Yellow Dog, say, "Good night!"

*Due to the number of cards that must be manipulated, this chart will be easier for children to manage if it is in a pocket chart.

8. Repeat the rhyme using the other describing words and animal words until the children can easily read the rhyme.
9. Place the interactive chart in the reading center, along with the describing word and animal word cards. You may want to place the cards for each animal, along with its corresponding description word card, into small, resealable plastic bags and label the bags with the animal word.
10. During center time, have children work with partners to change the animal and description words and read the chart. You may want to have a pointer at the center, so one child can be the "teacher" as he works with the other student.
11. Give each child a copy of the "Teddy Bear, Teddy Bear" take-home book (see pattern on pages 101-103) and let him illustrate it.
12. Once a student completes his take-home book, have him read the book to a classmate.
13. Send the take-home books home with the students, and have students read the books to their parents, grandparents, siblings, etc.

Oh, A-Hunting We Will Go

Preparation:
Make the "Oh, A-Hunting We Will Go" chart using either lined chart paper or sentence strips and a pocket chart.

Oh, A-Hunting We Will Go
Oh, a-hunting we will go,
A-hunting we will go.
We'll catch a fox
And put it in a box,
And then we'll let it go.

Also, write the animal words and rhyming place words on cards. Use the suggested words below or have children brainstorm a list of animal words and matching places.

pig – wig	mouse – house	cat – hat
dog – bog	eel – wheel	skunk – trunk
fish – dish	frog – log	bat – hat

Steps:

1. Introduce the interactive chart to students during "big group" time.
2. Read the original rhyme to the class several times.
3. Model how to replace the animal and rhyming place word in the rhyme with other words. For example, show how "fox" can be replaced by "pig" and "box" can be replaced by "wig." Then, read the new rhyme to and with the class.

   Oh, a-hunting we will go,
   A-hunting we will go,
   We'll catch a pig
   And put it in a wig,
   And then we'll let it go.
4. Repeat with additional animal and place words until the children can easily read the rhyme.
5. Place the interactive chart in the reading center, along with the animal and rhyming place cards.
6. During center time, have children work with partners to change the animal and place words and read the chart. You may want to have a pointer at the center, so one child can be the "teacher" as she works with the other student.
7. Give each child a copy of the "Oh, A-Hunting We Will Go" take-home book (see pattern on pages 105-106) and let her illustrate it.
8. Once a student completes her take-home book, have her read the book to a classmate.
9. Send the take-home books home with the students, and have students read the books to their parents, grandparents, siblings, etc.

Down in the Meadow

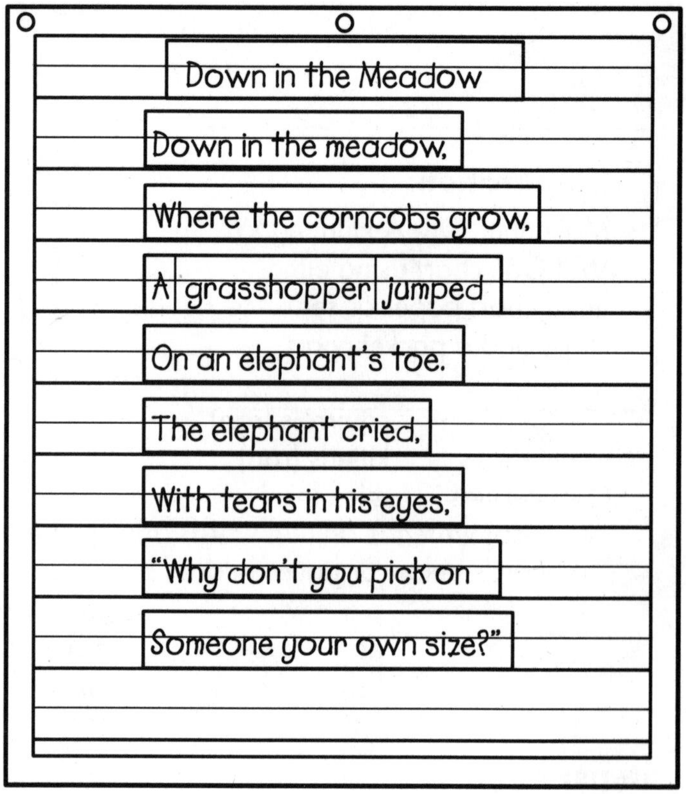
Down in the Meadow
Down in the meadow,
Where the corncobs grow,
A grasshopper jumped
On an elephant's toe.
The elephant cried,
With tears in his eyes,
"Why don't you pick on
Someone your own size?"

Preparation:
Make the "Down in the Meadow" chart using either lined chart paper or sentence strips and a pocket chart. Write small animal or bug names on word cards or pieces of sentence strips. Use the suggested words below or have children brainstorm a list of words.

ant beetle
bug mouse
bird ladybug

Steps:

1. Introduce the interactive chart to students during "big group" time.
2. Read the original rhyme to the class several times.
3. Model how to replace the animal/bug word in the rhyme with another word. For example, show how "grasshopper" can be replaced by "ant." Then, read the new rhyme to and with the class.

   Down in the meadow,
   Where the corncobs grow,
   An ant jumped
   On an elephant's toe.
   The elephant cried,
   With tears in his eyes,
   "Why don't you pick on
   Someone your own size?"

4. Repeat with additional animal or bug words until the children can easily read the rhyme.
5. Place the interactive chart in the reading center, along with the animal/bug cards.
6. During center time, have children work with partners to change the animal/bug words and read the chart. You may want to have a pointer at the center, so one child can be the "teacher" as he works with the other student.
7. Give each child a copy of the "Down in the Meadow" take-home book (see pattern on pages 107-108) and let him illustrate it.
8. Once a student completes his take-home book, have him read the book to a classmate.
9. Send the take-home books home with the students, and have students read the books to their parents, grandparents, siblings, etc.

Chickadees

Preparation:
Make the "Chickadees" chart using either lined chart paper or sentence strips and a pocket chart. Write other birds or small animal names on word cards or pieces of sentence strips. Use the words below or have children brainstorm a list of words. If the animal chosen by students doesn't fly, change "fly" to "ran."

robins	squirrels (ran)
blue jays	kittens (ran)
butterflies	mice (ran)

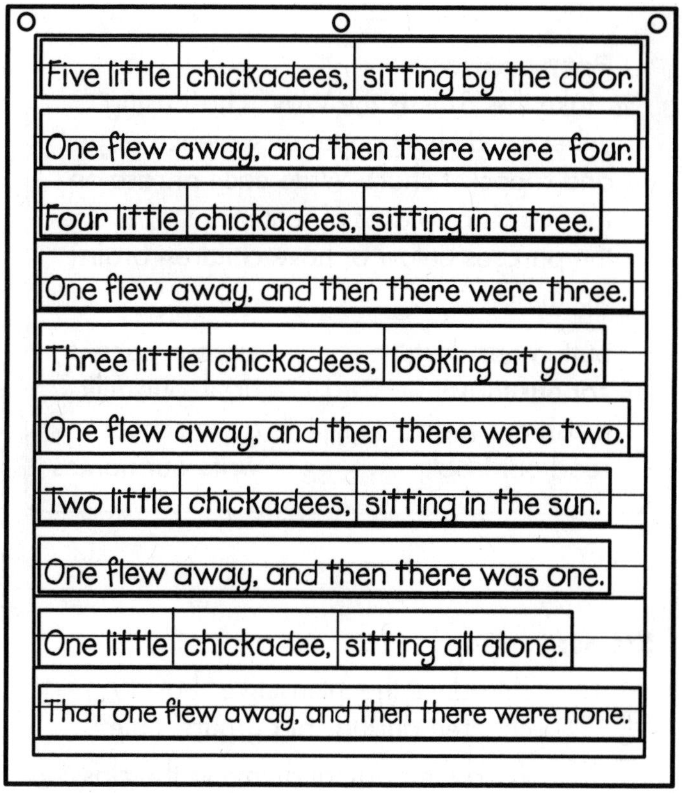
Five little chickadees, sitting by the door.
One flew away, and then there were four.
Four little chickadees, sitting in a tree.
One flew away, and then there were three.
Three little chickadees, looking at you.
One flew away, and then there were two.
Two little chickadees, sitting in the sun.
One flew away, and then there was one.
One little chickadee, sitting all alone.
That one flew away, and then there were none.

Steps:

1. Introduce the interactive chart to students during "big group" time.
2. Read the original rhyme to the class several times.
3. Model how to replace the animal word in the rhyme with another word. For example, show how "chickadees" can be replaced with "robins." Then, read the new rhyme to and with the class.
4. Repeat with additional animal words until the children can easily read the rhyme.
5. Place the interactive chart in the reading center, along with the bird/small animal cards. You may want to place the cards for each animal/bird in a small, resealable plastic bag and label the bag with the animal/bird word.
6. During center time, have children work with partners to change the animal word and read the chart. You may want to have a pointer at the center, so one child can be the "teacher" as she works with the other student.
7. Give each child a copy of the "Chickadees" take-home book (see pattern on pages 109-112) and let her illustrate it.
8. Once a student completes her take-home book, have her read the book to a classmate.
9. Send the take-home books home with the students, and have students read the books to their parents, grandparents, siblings, etc.

Five little robins, sitting by a door
One flew away, and then there were four.
Four little robins, sitting in a tree
One flew away, and then there were three.
Three little robins, looking at you
One flew away, and then there were two.
Two little robins, sitting in the sun
One flew away, and then there was one.
One little robin, sitting all alone
That one flew away, and then there were none.

This Is the Way

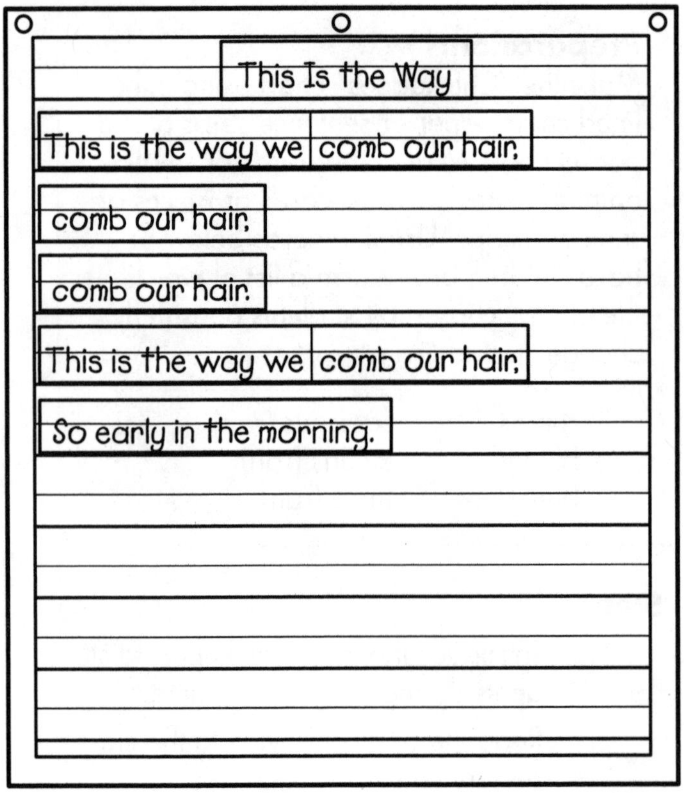
This Is the Way
This is the way we
comb our hair,
comb our hair,
comb our hair.
This is the way we
comb our hair,
So early in the morning.

Preparation:
Make the "This Is the Way" chart using either lined chart paper or sentence strips and a pocket chart. Write each phrase on four cards or pieces of sentence strips. Use the phrases below or have children brainstorm new ones.*

button our shirts	zip our pants
eat our toast	drink our milk
brush our teeth	go to school
read our books	write our names

Steps:

1. Introduce the interactive chart to children during "big group" time.
2. Read the original rhyme to the class several times.
3. Model how to replace the action in the rhyme with another action phrase. For example, show how "comb our hair" can be replaced with "button our shirts." Then, read the new rhyme to and with the class.

   This is the way we button our shirts, button our shirts, button our shirts.
   This is the way we button our shirts so early in the morning.
4. Repeat with additional phrases until the children can easily read the rhyme. You may want to place the cards for each phrase in a separate resealable plastic bag and label the bag with the phrase.
5. During center time, have children work with partners to change the phrases and read the chart. You may want to have a pointer at the center, so one child can be the "teacher" as he works with the other student.
6. Give each child a copy of the "This Is the Way" take-home book (see pattern on pages 113-114) and let him illustrate it.
7. Once a student completes his take-home book, have him read the book to a classmate.
8. Send the take-home books home with the students, and have students read the books to their parents, grandparents, siblings, etc.

*You can also name things that are done in the classroom on a daily basis. For example:
This is the way we go to art, go to art, go to art.
This is the way we go to art so early in the morning.

Roses Are Red

Preparation:
Make the "Roses Are Red" chart using either lined chart paper or sentence strips and a pocket chart.

Roses Are Red

Roses are red,
Violets are blue,
Sugar is sweet,
And so are you.

Write things that are red, blue, and sweet on word cards or pieces of sentence strips. Use the words below or have children brainstorm new ones.

Hearts	Skies
Honey	Stop signs
Oceans	Candy

Steps:

1. Introduce the interactive chart to students during "big group" time.
2. Read the original rhyme to the class several times.
3. Model how to replace the words in the rhyme with other words. For example, show how "Roses" can be replaced with "Hearts," "Violets" can be replaced with "Skies," and "Sugar" can be replaced with "Honey." Then, read the new rhyme to and with the class.

   Hearts are red,
   Skies are blue,
   Honey is sweet,
   And so are you.
4. Repeat with additional words until the children can easily read the rhyme.
5. Place the interactive chart in the reading center, along with the word cards.
6. During center time, have children work with partners to change the words and read the chart. You may want to have a pointer at the center, so one child can be the "teacher" as he works with the other student.
7. Give each child a copy of the "Roses Are Red" take-home book (see pattern on pages 113-114) and let her illustrate it.
8. Once a student completes her take-home book, have her read the book to a classmate.
9. Send the take-home books home with the students, and have students read the books to their parents, grandparents, siblings, etc.

Books

Preparation:
Make the "Books" chart using lined chart paper or sentence strips and a pocket chart. Write some of your students' favorite story characters and some words your students use to describe them on word cards or pieces of sentence strips.

Example:

Books

I like Clifford.
He is big.
The stories are funny.
I like books.

Books

I like ________________.
________ is ____________.
The stories are __________.
I like books!

Steps:

1. Introduce the interactive chart to students during "big group" time. This might follow the reading of three different books about three different characters.
2. Read the chart to them using one book character and the words the children chose to describe the character.
3. Read the chart again and let the children be your echo. Read it a third time with the children joining in and sharing the reading (shared reading).
4. Model how to replace the name of this character with another character's name and then change the next two sentences.
5. Have the children read this new chart to you.
6. Place the interactive chart in the reading center, along with the character and description cards. You may want to place these cards in three separate resealable plastic bags—one for the book characters, one for words describing the characters, and one for words describing the stories.
7. During center time, have children work with partners to change the words and read the chart. You may want to have a pointer at the center, so one child can be the "teacher" as he works with other student.
8. Give each child a copy of the "Books" take-home book (see pattern on pages 117-118) and let him illustrate it.
9. Once a student completes his take-home book, have him read the book to a classmate.
10. Send the take-home books home with the students, and have students read the books to their parents, grandparents, siblings, etc.

Me

Preparation:
Make the "Me" chart using either lined chart paper or sentence strips and a pocket chart. Prepare several word cards or sentence strips for recording student responses.

Me
My eyes are ______________.
My hair is ______________.
My smile is ______________.
I am ______________.
I am just right!

Steps:

1. Introduce the blank interactive theme chart to students during "big group" time. Use the chart to interview several children for their responses.

   Examples:
   blue, brown, green, hazel
   brown, blonde, black, red, strawberry blonde
   bright, big, happy, sunny
   tall, thin, big, short

2. Write their answers on word cards or pieces of sentence strips.
3. Model how to place the word cards over the blanks in the chart. Read the completed chart with the class.

   My eyes are blue.
   My hair is red.
   My smile is bright.
   I am short.
   I am just right!

4. Repeat with additional words until the children can easily read the chart.
5. Place the interactive chart in the reading center, along with the students' word cards. Add any choices that might be necessary.
6. Students can complete the interactive chart during center time, using their information or a friend's information. Once the chart is complete, have the student read the chart to someone in the center.
7. Give each child a copy of the "Me" take-home book (see pattern on pages 119-120) and let her illustrate it.
8. Once a student completes her take-home book, have her read the book to a classmate.
9. Send the take-home books home with the students, and have students read the books to their parents, grandparents, siblings, etc.

My Family

Preparation:
Make the "My Family" chart using either lined chart paper or sentence strips and a pocket chart. Prepare several word cards or sentence strips for recording student responses.

My Family
I have ____________ people in my family.
I am the ______________________.
We live in a ______________________.
We like to ________________ together.

Steps:

1. Introduce the blank interactive theme chart to students during "big group" time. Use the chart to interview several children for their responses.

Examples:
two, three, four, ten
oldest, youngest, middle child, only child
house, apartment, trailer, duplex
read books, go to the park, talk, play games

2. Write their answers on word cards or pieces of sentence strips.
3. Model how to place the word cards over the blanks in the chart. Read the completed chart with the class.

   I have two people in my family.
   I am the youngest.
   We live in a house.
   We like to read books together.
4. Repeat with additional words/phrases until the children can easily read the chart.
5. Place the interactive chart in the reading center, along with the students' word cards. Add any choices that might be necessary.
6. Students can complete the interactive chart during center time, using their information or their friends' information. Once the chart is complete, have students read the chart to someone in the center.
7. Give each child a copy of the "My Family" take-home book (see pattern on pages 121-122) and let him illustrate it.
8. Once a student completes his take-home book, have him read the book to a classmate.
9. Send the take-home books home with the students, and have students read the books to their parents, grandparents, siblings, etc.

Friends

Preparation:
Make the "Friends" chart using either lined chart paper or sentence strips and a pocket chart. Prepare several word cards or sentence strips for recording student responses.

Friends
I have ______________ friends.
We like to ______________.
A good friend ______________.
I am glad I have friends.

Steps:

1. Introduce the blank interactive theme chart to students during "big group" time. Use the chart to interview several children for their responses.

   Examples:
   three, ten, twelve, fifteen
   ride bikes, read books, sleep over
   cares, hugs, laughs, plays with me, listens

2. Write their answers on word cards or pieces of sentence strips.
3. Model how to place the word cards over the blanks in the chart. Read the completed chart with the class.

   I have three friends.
   We like to ride bikes.
   A good friend cares.
   I am glad I have friends.

4. Repeat with additional words/phrases until the children can easily read the chart.
5. Place the interactive chart in the reading center, along with the students' word cards. Add any choices that might be necessary.
6. Students can complete the interactive chart during center time, using their information or their friends' information. Once the chart is complete, have students read the chart to someone in the center.
7. Give each child a copy of the "Friends" take-home book (see pattern on pages 123-124) and let her illustrate it.
8. Once a student completes her take-home book, have her read the book to a classmate.
9. Send the take-home books home with the students, and have students read the books to their parents, grandparents, siblings, etc.

My Body

Preparation:
Make the "My Body" chart using either lined chart paper or sentence strips and a pocket chart. Prepare several word cards or sentence strips for recording student responses.

My Body
My body is very special.
I have ________, ________, and ________.
The most useful part of my body ________.
I like ________________ best because
________________________________.

Steps:

1. Introduce the blank interactive theme chart to students during "big group" time. Use the chart to interview several children for their responses.

   Examples:
   arms, legs, hands, feet, eyes
   are my hands, are my feet, are my eyes, are my fingers
   my eyes, they help me see; my hands, they help me feel

2. Write their answers on word cards or pieces of sentence strips.
3. Model how to place the word cards over the blanks in the chart. Read the completed chart with the class.

   My body is very special.
   I have arms, legs, and hands.
   The most useful part of my body are my eyes.
   I like my eyes best because they help me see.
4. Repeat with additional words/phrases until the children can easily read the chart.
5. Place the interactive chart in the reading center, along with the students' word cards. Add any choices that might be necessary.
6. Students can complete the interactive chart during center time, using their information or their friends' information. Once the chart is complete, have students read the chart to someone in the center.
7. Give each child a copy of the "My Body" take-home book (see pattern on pages 125-126) and let him illustrate it.
8. Once a student completes his take-home book, have him read the book to a classmate.
9. Send the take-home books home with the students, and have students read the books to their parents, grandparents, siblings, etc.

Clothing

Preparation:
Make the "Clothing" chart using either lined chart paper or sentence strips and a pocket chart. Prepare several cards or sentence strips for recording student responses.

Clothing
I wear clothes.
I have on a ________________.
I have on ________________.
I wear ________________ shoes.
My clothes keep me ________________.

Steps:

1. Introduce the blank interactive theme chart to students during "big group" time. Use the chart to interview several children for their responses.

   Examples:
   blue top, black jacket, yellow blouse, green shirt
   black pants, blue jeans, pink hose, red socks
   dress, white, new, old, tennis
   clean, dry, cool, warm

2. Write their answers on word cards or pieces of sentence strips.
3. Model how to place the word cards over the blanks in the chart. Read the completed chart with the class.

   I wear clothes.
   I have on a green shirt.
   I have on red socks.
   I wear tennis shoes.
   My clothes keep me warm.

4. Repeat with additional words/phrases until the children can easily read the chart.
5. Place the interactive chart in the reading center, along with the students' word cards. Add any choices that might be necessary.
6. Students can complete the interactive chart during center time, using their information or their friends' information. Once the chart is complete, have students read the chart to someone in the center.
7. Give each child a copy of the "Clothing" take-home book (see pattern on pages 127-128) and let her illustrate it.
8. Once a student completes her take-home book, have her read the book to a classmate.
9. Send the take-home books home with the students, and have students read the books to their parents, grandparents, siblings, etc.

Rainbows

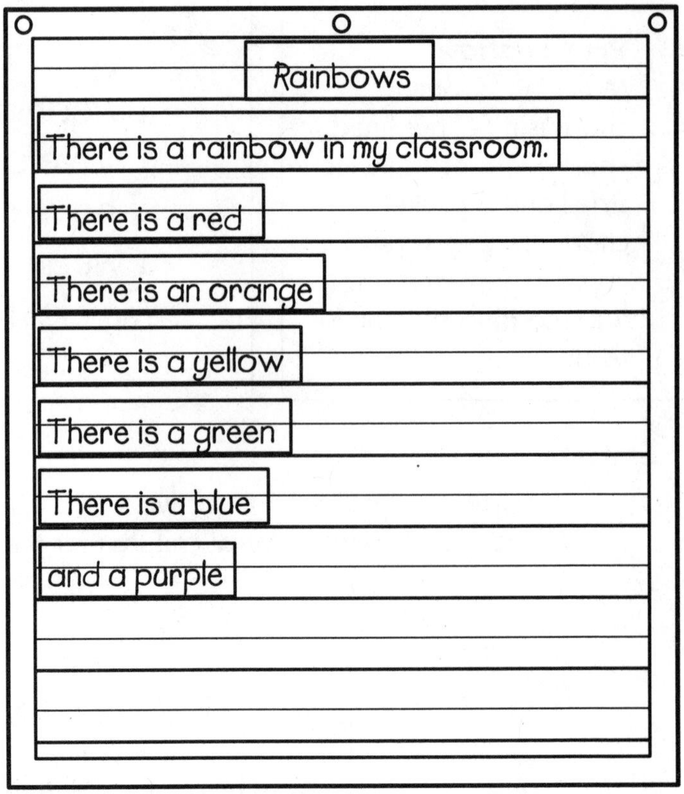
Rainbows
There is a rainbow in my classroom.
There is a red
There is an orange
There is a yellow
There is a green
There is a blue
and a purple

Preparation:
Make the "Rainbows" chart using either lined chart paper or sentence strips and a pocket chart. Prepare several word cards or sentence strips for recording student responses.

Steps:

1. Introduce the blank interactive theme chart to students during "big group" time. Use the chart to interview several children for their responses. Ask them to identify things in the classroom* that match the colors in the rainbow.
2. Write their answers on word cards or pieces of sentence strips.
3. Model how to place the word cards over the blanks in the chart. Read the completed chart with the class.

   There is a rainbow in my classroom.
   There is a red chair.
   There is an orange pumpkin.
   There is a yellow pencil.
   There is a green plant.
   There is a blue coat,
   and a purple notebook.
4. Repeat with additional words until the children can easily read the chart.
5. Place the interactive chart in the reading center, along with the students' word cards. Add any choices that might be necessary.
6. Students can complete the interactive chart during center time. Once the chart is complete, have students read the chart to someone in the center.
7. Give each child a copy of the "Rainbows" take-home book (see pattern on pages 127-128) and let him illustrate it.
8. Once a student completes his take-home book, have him read the book to a classmate.
9. Send the take-home books home with the students, and have students read the books to their parents, grandparents, siblings, etc.

*There are other places where children can find rainbows. You can use the same chart by replacing the location (neighborhood, closet, garden, farm, etc.).

Post Office

Preparation:
Make the "Post Office" chart using either lined chart paper or sentence strips and a pocket chart. Prepare several word cards or sentence strips for recording student responses.

Post Office
You mail a ______________________.
The mail carrier delivers it to your __________.
Your ____________________ is so happy,
__________ sends you a ______________.
And the mail carrier delivers it to you.

Steps:

1. Introduce the blank interactive theme chart to students during "big group" time. Use the chart to interview several children for their responses.

   Examples:
   letter, package, postcard, birthday card, Valentine
   grandmother, grandfather, sister, cousin, friend
   grandmother, she, letter; sister, she, package; friend, he, postcard

2. Write their answers on word cards or pieces of sentence strips.
3. Model how to place the word cards over the blanks in the chart. Read the completed chart with the class.

   You mail a letter.
   The mail carrier delivers it to your friend.
   Your friend is so happy, she sends you a postcard.
   And the mail carrier delivers it to you.

4. Repeat with additional words/phrases until the children can easily read the chart.
5. Place the interactive chart in the reading center, along with the students' word cards. Add any choices that might be necessary.
6. Students can complete the interactive chart during center time, using their information or their friends' information. Once the chart is complete, have students read the chart to someone in the center.
7. Give each child a copy of the "Post Office" take-home book (see pattern on pages 131-132) and let her illustrate it.
8. Once a student completes her take-home book, have her read the book to a classmate.
9. Send the take-home books home with the students, and have students read the books to their parents, grandparents, siblings, etc.

Travel

Preparation:
Make the "Travel" chart using either lined chart paper or sentence strips and a pocket chart. Prepare several word cards or sentence strips for recording student responses.

Travel
We're going on a trip.
We will take a ________.
We will stay in a ________.
When we get there, we will ________.

Steps:

1. Introduce the blank interactive theme chart to students during "big group" time. Use the chart to interview several children for their responses. Ask them to tell you about places they travel to and ways they get there.

   Examples:
   plane, car, bus, bike, motorcycle
   hotel, motel, tent, house
   see a show, play, go to the zoo, see Mickey Mouse

2. Write their answers on word cards or pieces of sentence strips.
3. Model how to place the word cards over the blanks in the chart. Read the completed chart with the class.

   We're going on a trip.
   We will take a plane.
   We will stay in a hotel.
   When we get there, we will see a show.

4. Repeat with additional words/phrases until the children can easily read the chart.
5. Place the interactive chart in the reading center, along with the students' word cards. Add any choices that might be necessary.
6. Students can complete the interactive chart during center time, using their information or their friends' information. Once the chart is complete, have students read the chart to someone in the center.
7. Give each child a copy of the "Travel" take-home book (see pattern on pages 133-134) and let him illustrate it.
8. Once a student completes his take-home book, have him read the book to a classmate.
9. Send the take-home books home with the students, and have students read the books to their parents, grandparents, siblings, etc.

Doctor's Office

Preparation:
Make the "Doctor's Office" chart using either lined chart paper or sentence strips and a pocket chart. Prepare several word cards or sentence strips for recording student responses.

Doctor's Office
I go to see the doctor.
My doctor is ________.
My doctor gives me ________.
My doctor tells me to ________.

Steps:

1. Introduce the blank interactive theme chart to students during "big group" time. Use the chart to interview several children for their responses.

   Examples:
   nice, tall, young
   stickers, shots, medicine
   eat good food, sleep, listen to Mom, take my medicine

2. Write their answers on word cards or pieces of sentence strips.
3. Model how to place the word cards over the blanks in the chart. Read the completed chart with the class.

   I go to see the doctor.
   My doctor is nice.
   My doctor gives me stickers.
   My doctor tells me to eat good food.
4. Repeat with additional words/phrases until the children can easily read the chart.
5. Place the interactive chart in the reading center, along with additional word cards. Add any choices that might be necessary.
6. Students can complete the interactive chart during center time, using their information or their friends' information. Once the chart is complete have students read the chart to someone in the center.
7. Give each child a copy of the "Doctor's Office" take-home book (see pattern on pages 133-134) and let her illustrate it.
8. Once a student completes her take-home book, have her read the book to a classmate.
9. Send the take-home books home with the students, and have students read the books to their parents, grandparents, siblings, etc.

Grocery Store

Preparation:
Make the "Grocery Store" chart using either lined chart paper or sentence strips and a pocket chart. Prepare several word cards or sentence strips for recording student responses.

Grocery Store
The grocery store is a neat place.
It has ________.
When I go, I ________.
The best part of the grocery store is ________.

Steps:

1. Introduce the blank interactive theme chart to students during "big group" time. Use the chart to interview several children for their responses.

   Examples:
   food, fruit, vegetables, cookies
   buy food, push the cart, ride in the cart, choose dinner, get candy
   choosing dinner, the food, the cart, the candy

2. Write their answers on word cards or pieces of sentence strips.
3. Model how to place the word cards over the blanks in the chart. Read the completed chart with the class.

   The grocery store is a neat place.
   It has good food.
   When I go, I push the cart.
   The best part of the grocery store is choosing dinner.

4. Repeat with additional words/phrases until the children can easily read the chart.
5. Place the interactive chart in the reading center, along with the word cards. Add any choices that might be necessary.
6. Students can complete the interactive chart during center time, using their information or their friends' information. Once the chart is complete, have students read the chart to someone in the center.
7. Give each child a copy of the "Grocery Store" take-home book (see pattern on pages 137-138) and let him illustrate it.
8. Once a student completes his take-home book, have him read the book to a classmate.
9. Send the take-home books home with the students, and have students read the books to their parents, grandparents, siblings, etc.

Restaurants

Preparation:
Make the "Restaurants" chart using either lined chart paper or sentence strips and a pocket chart. Prepare several word cards or sentence strips for recording student responses.

Restaurants
We go out to eat.
We go to ____________.
We order ____________.
I drink ____________.

Steps:

1. Introduce the blank interactive theme chart to students during "big group" time. Use the chart to interview several children for their responses.

   Examples:
   Taco Bell®, McDonalds®, Pizza Hut®, Chili's®
   tacos, hamburgers, pizza, chicken
   Coke®, Pepsi®, Dr. Pepper®, Mountain Dew®, orange soda

47

2. Write their answers on word cards or pieces of sentence strips.
3. Model how to place the word cards over the blanks in the chart. Read the completed chart with the class.

   We go out to eat.
   We go to Taco Bell®.
   We order tacos.
   I drink orange soda.
4. Repeat with additional words/phrases until the children can easily read the chart.
5. Place the interactive chart in the reading center, along with the word cards. Add any choices that might be necessary.
6. Students can complete the interactive chart during center time, using their information or their friends' information. Once the chart is complete have students read the chart to someone in the center.
7. Give each child a copy of the "Restaurants" take-home book (see pattern on pages 139-140) and let her illustrate it.
8. Once a student completes her take-home book, have her read the book to a classmate.
9. Send the take-home books home with the students, and have students read the books to their parents, grandparents, siblings, etc.

Grandparents' Day

Preparation:
Make the "Grandparents' Day" chart using either lined chart paper or sentence strips and a pocket chart. Prepare several word cards or sentence strips for recording student responses.

Grandparents' Day
My grandfather and I ________.
My grandmother and I ________.
I see my grandparents ________.
My grandparents ________!

Steps:

1. Introduce the blank interactive theme chart to students during "big group" time. Use the chart to interview several children for their responses.

   Examples:
   play, read, travel
   make dinner, bake cookies, play games
   at Thanksgiving, at Christmas, every day
   are great, take good care of me, love me

2. Write their answers on word cards or pieces of sentence strips in the chart.
3. Model how to place the word cards over the blanks in the chart. Read the completed chart with the class.

   My grandfather and I play.
   My grandmother and I bake cookies.
   I see my grandparents every day.
   My grandparents take good care of me!

4. Repeat with additional words/phrases until the children can easily read the chart.
5. Place the interactive chart in the reading center, along with the word cards. Add any choices that might be necessary.
6. Students can complete the interactive chart during center time, using their information or their friends' information. Once the chart is complete have students read the chart to someone in the center.
7. Give each child a copy of the "Grandparents' Day" take-home book (see pattern on pages 141-142) and let him illustrate it.
8. Once a student completes his take-home book, have him read the book to a classmate.
9. Send the take-home books home with the students, and have students read the books to their parents, grandparents, siblings, etc.

Presidents' Day

Preparation:
Make the "Presidents' Day" chart using either lined chart paper or sentence strips and a pocket chart. Prepare several cards or sentence strips for recording student responses.

Presidents' Day
Presidents' Day is ____________.
Presidents ____________.
They ____________.
President ____________ is our president.
On Presidents' Day we remember ____________.

Steps:

1. Introduce the blank interactive theme chart to students during "big group" time. Use the chart to interview several children for their responses.

   Examples:
   a holiday, a special day to remember
   run the country, are important, are special people
   make important decisions, make laws, take care of us
   George Washington, Abraham Lincoln

2. Write their answers on word cards or pieces of sentence strips in the chart.
3. Model how to place the word cards over the blanks in the chart. Read the completed chart with the class.

   Presidents' Day is a day to remember.
   Presidents run the country.
   They make important decisions.
   President Bush is our president.
   On Presidents' Day we remember George Washington.

4. Repeat with additional words/phrases until the children can easily read the chart.
5. Place the interactive chart in the reading center, along with the word cards. Add any choices that might be necessary.
6. Students can complete the interactive chart during center time, using their information or their friends' information. Once the chart is complete have students read the chart to someone in the center.
7. Give each child a copy of the "Presidents' Day" take-home book (see pattern on pages 143-144) and let her illustrate it.
8. Once a student completes her take-home book, have her read the book to a classmate.
9. Send the take-home books home with the students, and have students read the books to their parents, grandparents, siblings, etc.

Bugs

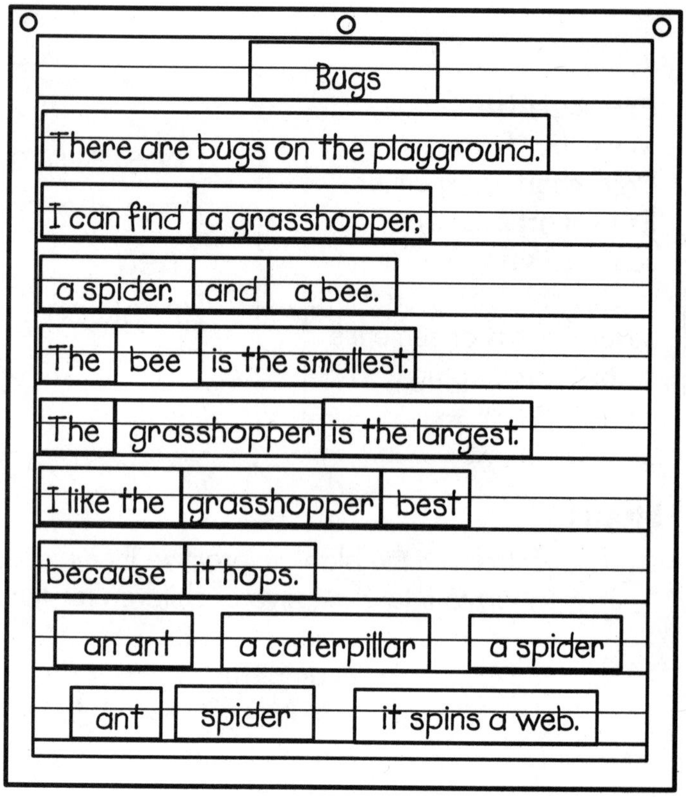

Preparation:
Make the "Bugs" chart using either lined chart paper or sentence strips and a pocket chart. Prepare several word cards or sentence strips for recording student responses.

Steps:

1. Introduce the blank interactive theme chart to students during "big group" time. Use the chart to interview several children for their responses (see the chart at right for examples).
2. Write their answers on word cards or pieces of sentence strips in the chart.
3. Model how to place the word cards over the blanks in the chart. Read the completed chart with the class.

   There are bugs on the playground.
   I can find an ant, a spider, and a bee.
   The ant is the smallest.
   The spider is the largest.
   I like the bee best because it can fly.
4. Repeat with additional words/phrases until the children can easily read the chart.
5. Place the interactive chart in the reading center, along with the word cards. Add any choices that might be necessary.
6. Students can complete the interactive chart during center time, using their information or their friends' information. Once the chart is complete have students read the chart to someone in the center.
7. Give each child a copy of the "Bugs" take-home book (see pattern on pages 145-146) and let him illustrate it.
8. Once a student completes his take-home book, have him read the book to a classmate.
9. Send the take-home books home with the students, and have students read the books to their parents, grandparents, siblings, etc.

Birds

Preparation:
Make the "Birds" chart using either lined chart paper or sentence strips and a pocket chart. Prepare several word cards or sentence strips for recording student responses.

Birds
We see birds in the trees.
They have ________________.
Some are ________________.
They eat ________________.

Steps:

1. Introduce the blank interactive theme chart to students during "big group" time. Use the chart to interview several children for their responses.

   Examples:
   wings, beaks, eyes, claws
   black, blue, red, big, little
   worms, seeds, nuts

2. Write their answers on word cards or pieces of sentence strips in the chart.
3. Model how to place the word cards over the blanks in the chart. Read the completed chart with the class.

   We see birds in the trees.
   They have wings.
   Some are black.
   They eat worms.

4. Repeat with additional words until the children can easily read the chart.
5. Place the interactive chart in the reading center, along with the word cards. Add any choices that might be necessary.
6. Students can complete the interactive chart during center time, using their information or their friends' information. Once the chart is complete have students read the chart to some-one in the center.
7. Give each child a copy of the "Birds" take-home book (see pattern on pages 147-148) and let her illustrate it.
8. Once a student completes her take-home book, have her read the book to a classmate.
9. Send the take-home books home with the students, and have students read the books to their parents, grandparents, siblings, etc.

Frogs and Toads

Preparation:
Make the "Frogs and Toads" chart using either lined chart paper or sentence strips and a pocket chart. Prepare several word cards or sentence strips for recording student responses.

Frogs and Toads
Frogs and toads are ________.
Frogs are ________.
They live ________.
Toads are ________.
They live ________.

Steps:

1. Introduce the blank interactive theme chart to students during "big group" time. Use the chart to interview several children for their responses.

   Examples:
   green, animals, small, cute
   wet, smooth, slimy
   in water, near water
   dry, bumpy, loud
   on land, near water

2. Write their answers on word cards or pieces of sentence strips in the chart.
3. Model how to place the word cards over the blanks in the chart. Read the completed chart with the class.

   Frogs and toads are green.
   Frogs are wet.
   They live in water.
   Toads are dry.
   They live on land.

4. Repeat with additional words/phrases until the children can easily read the chart.
5. Place the interactive chart in the reading center, along with the word cards. Add any choices that might be necessary.
6. Students can complete the interactive chart during center time, using their information or their friends' information. Once the chart is complete have students read the chart to someone in the center.
7. Give each child a copy of the "Frogs and Toads" take-home book (see pattern on pages 149-150) and let him illustrate it.
8. Once a student completes his take-home book, have him read the book to a classmate.
9. Send the take-home books home with the students, and have students read the books to their parents, grandparents, siblings, etc.

Pets

Preparation:
Make the "Pets" chart using either lined chart paper or sentence strips and a pocket chart. Prepare several word cards or sentence strips for recording student responses.

Pets
Pets are great.
________________ are pets.
They eat ________________.
They ________________.

Steps:

1. Introduce the blank interactive theme chart to students during "big group" time. Use the chart to interview several children for their responses.

   Examples:
   Cats, Dogs, Gerbils
   cat food, dog food, seeds
   purr, bark, run

2. Write their answers on word cards or pieces of sentence strips in the chart.
3. Model how to place the word cards over the blanks in the chart. Read the completed chart with the class.

   Pets are great.
   Cats are pets.
   They eat cat food.
   They purr.

4. Repeat with additional words until the children can easily read the chart.
5. Place the interactive chart in the reading center, along with the word cards. Add any choices that might be necessary.
6. Students can complete the interactive chart during center time, using their information or their friends' information. Once the chart is complete have students read the chart to some-one in the center.
7. Give each child a copy of the "Pets" take-home book (see pattern on pages 151-152) and let her illustrate it.
8. Once a student completes her take-home book, have her read the book to a classmate.
9. Send the take-home books home with the students, and have students read the books to their parents, grandparents, siblings, etc.

Winter

Preparation:
Make the "Winter" chart using either lined chart paper or sentence strips and a pocket chart. Prepare several word cards or sentence strips for recording student responses.

Winter
It is winter.
In the winter, it ______________________.
We ______________________________.
We wear ________________________.
Winter is great because _____________.

Steps:

1. Introduce the blank interactive theme chart to students during "big group" time. Use the chart to interview several children for their responses.

   Examples:
   snows, is cold, gets dark early
   play in the snow, make snowmen
   coats, hats, scarves, mittens, gloves
   it is Christmas time, it snows, we can play in the snow

2. Write their answers on word cards or pieces of sentence strips.
3. Model how to place the word cards over the blanks in the chart. Read the completed chart with the class.

   It is winter.
   In the winter, it snows.
   We play in the snow.
   We wear coats.
   Winter is great because it is Christmas time.

4. Repeat with additional words/phrases until the children can easily read the chart.
5. Place the interactive chart in the reading center, along with the word cards. Add any choices that might be necessary.
6. Students can complete the interactive chart during center time, using their information or their friends' information. Once the chart is complete, have students read the chart to someone in the center.
7. Give each child a copy of the "Winter" take-home book (see pattern on pages 153-154) and let her illustrate it.
8. Once a student completes her take-home book, have her read the book to a classmate.
9. Send the take-home books home with the students, and have students read the books to their parents, grandparents, siblings, etc.

Spring

Preparation:
Make the "Spring" chart using either lined chart paper or sentence strips and a pocket chart. Prepare several word cards or sentence strips for recording student responses.

Spring
It is spring.
In the spring, ________________.
We ________________.
We wear ________________.
Spring is great because ________________.

Steps:

1. Introduce the blank interactive theme chart to students during "big group" time. Use the chart to interview several children for their responses.

   Examples:
   it rains, flowers bloom, it gets warm
   play outside, plant flowers, pick flowers
   raincoats, shorts, rain boots
   flowers grow, we can play outside, we don't have to wear our coats

2. Write their answers on word cards or pieces of sentence strips.
3. Model how to place the word cards over the blanks in the chart. Read the completed chart with the class.

   It is spring.
   In the spring, it rains.
   We play outside.
   We wear raincoats.
   Spring is great because flowers grow.

4. Repeat with additional words/phrases until the children can easily read the chart.
5. Place the interactive chart in the reading center, along with the word cards. Add any choices that might be necessary.
6. Students can complete the interactive chart during center time, using their information or their friends' information. Once the chart is complete, have students read the chart to someone in the center.
7. Give each child a copy of the "Spring" take-home book (see pattern on pages 155-156) and let him illustrate it.
8. Once a student completes his take-home book, have him read the book to a classmate.
9. Send the take-home books home with the students, and have students read the books to their parents, grandparents, siblings, etc.

Summer

Preparation:
Make the "Summer" chart using either lined chart paper or sentence strips and a pocket chart. Prepare several word cards or sentence strips for recording student responses.

Summer
Soon it will be summer.
In the summer, it is ______________.
We ______________________.
We play ____________________.
Summer is great because ______.

Steps:

1. Introduce the blank interactive theme chart to students during "big group" time. Use the chart to interview several children for their responses.

Examples:
hot, sunny, fun
go swimming, don't go to school, ride bikes
outside, baseball, soccer, all day
we take vacations, we celebrate Fourth of July

2. Write their answers on word cards or pieces of sentence strips.
3. Model how to place the word cards over the blanks in the chart. Read the completed chart with the class.

   Soon it will be summer.
   In the summer, it is hot.
   We go swimming.
   We play outside.
   Summer is great because we take vacations.
4. Repeat with additional words/phrases until the children can easily read the chart.
5. Place the interactive chart in the reading center, along with the word cards. Add any choices that might be necessary.
6. Students can complete the interactive chart during center time, using their information or their friends' information. Once the chart is complete, have students read the chart to someone in the center.
7. Give each child a copy of the "Summer" take-home book (see pattern on pages 157-158) and let her illustrate it.
8. Once a student completes her take-home book, have her read the book to a classmate.
9. Send the take-home books home with the students, and have students read the books to their parents, grandparents, siblings, etc.

Fall

Preparation:
Make the "Fall" chart using either lined chart paper or sentence strips and a pocket chart. Prepare several word cards or sentence strips for recording student responses.

Fall
After summer comes fall.
In the fall, ______________.
The leaves ______________.
We ______________.
Fall is great because ______________.

Steps:

1. Introduce the blank interactive theme chart to students during "big group" time. Use the chart to interview several children for their responses.

   Examples:
   it gets cold, days get shorter, it is football season
   turn colors, fall from the trees
   go back to school, watch football
   it is Halloween, it is Thanksgiving, we go back to school

2. Write their answers on word cards or pieces of sentence strips.
3. Model how to place the word cards over the blanks in the chart. Read the completed chart with the class.

   After summer comes fall.
   In the fall, it gets cold.
   The leaves turn colors.
   We go back to school.
   Fall is great because it is Halloween.

4. Repeat with additional words/phrases until the children can easily read the chart.
5. Place the interactive chart in the reading center, along with the word cards. Add any choices that might be necessary.
6. Students can complete the interactive chart during center time, using their information or their friends' information. Once the chart is complete, have students read the chart to someone in the center.
7. Give each child a copy of the "Fall" take-home book (see pattern on pages 159-160) and let him illustrate it.
8. Once a student completes his take-home book, have him read the book to a classmate.
9. Send the take-home books home with the students, and have students read the books to their parents, grandparents, siblings, etc.

Rocks

Preparation:
Make the "Rocks" chart using either lined chart paper or sentence strips and a pocket chart. Prepare several cards or sentence strips for recording student responses.

Rocks
The earth is made of rocks.
Rocks are ________.
Rocks can be ________.
Rocks can be ________.
We use rocks to build ________.

Steps:

1. Introduce the blank interactive theme chart to students during "big group" time. Use the chart to interview several children for their responses.

   Examples:
   hard, shiny, pretty
   red, gray, different colors
   big, little, round
   houses, walls, fireplaces, roads

2. Write their answers on individual word cards or sentence strips.
3. Model how to place the word cards over the blanks in the chart. Read the completed chart with the class.

   The earth is made of rocks.
   Rocks are hard.
   Rocks can be different colors.
   Rocks can be big.
   We use rocks to build houses.
4. Repeat with additional words/phrases until the children can easily read the chart.
5. Place the interactive chart in the reading center, along with the word cards. Add any choices that might be necessary.
6. Students can complete the interactive chart during center time, using their information or their friends' information. Once the chart is complete, have students read the chart to someone in the center.
7. Give each child a copy of the "Rocks" take-home book (see pattern on pages 161-162) and let her illustrate it.
8. Once a student completes her take-home book, have her read the book to a classmate.
9. Send the take-home books home with the students, and have students read the books to their parents, grandparents, siblings, etc.

Sun and Moon

Preparation:
Make the "Sun and Moon" chart using either lined chart paper or sentence strips and a pocket chart. Prepare several word cards or sentence strips for recording student responses.

Sun and Moon
The sun and moon are in the sky.
The sun ____________________.
It ____________________.
The moon ____________________.
It ____________________.

Steps:

1. Introduce the blank interactive theme chart to students during "big group" time. Use the chart to interview several children for their responses.

   Examples:
   is hot, is yellow, is bright
   shines during the day, gives us light
   is white, is full, is pretty
   shines at night, changes shape

2. Write their answers on word cards or pieces of sentence strips.
3. Model how to place the word cards over the blanks in the chart. Read the completed chart with the class.

   The sun and moon are in the sky.
   The sun is yellow.
   It shines during the day.
   The moon is white.
   It shines at night.

4. Repeat with additional words/phrases until the children can easily read the chart.
5. Place the interactive chart in the reading center, along with the word cards. Add any choices that might be necessary.
6. Students can complete the interactive chart during center time, using their information or their friends' information. Once the chart is complete, have students read the chart to someone in the center.
7. Give each child a copy of the "Sun and Moon" take-home book (see pattern on pages 163-164) and let him illustrate it.
8. Once a student completes his take-home book, have him read the book to a classmate.
9. Send the take-home books home with the students, and have students read the books to their parents, grandparents, siblings, etc.

The Sky

Preparation:
Make the"The Sky" chart using either lined chart paper or sentence strips and a pocket chart. Prepare several word cards or sentence strips for recording student responses.

The Sky
The sky is all around us.
Sometimes it is ____________________.
____________________ falls from the sky.
____________________ fly through the sky.
We get air to breathe from the sky.

Steps:

1. Introduce the blank interactive theme chart to students during "big group" time. Use the chart to interview several children for their responses.

    Examples:
    blue, gray, dark
    Snow, Rain, Sleet
    Birds, Planes, Butterflies, Bees

2. Write their answers on word cards or pieces of sentence strips.
3. Model how to place the word cards over the blanks in the chart. Read the completed chart with the class.

    The sky is all around us.
    Sometimes it is blue.
    Snow falls from the sky.
    Birds fly through the sky.
    We get air to breathe from the sky.

4. Repeat with additional words until the children can easily read the chart.
5. Place the interactive chart in the reading center, along with the word cards. Add any choices that might be necessary.
6. Students can complete the interactive chart during center time, using their information or their friends' information. Once the chart is complete, have students read the chart to someone in the center.
7. Give each child a copy of the "The Sky" take-home book (see pattern on pages 165-166) and let her illustrate it.
8. Once a student completes her take-home book, have her read the book to a classmate.
9. Send the take-home books home with the students, and have students read the books to their parents, grandparents, siblings, etc.

Plants

Preparation:
Make the "Plants" chart using either lined chart paper or sentence strips and a pocket chart. Prepare several word cards or sentence strips for recording student responses.

Plants
We see plants on our Earth.
I will plant ______________.
I will need a ______________.
Plants need ______________.
Plants need ______________.

Steps:

1. Introduce the blank interactive theme chart to students during "big group" time. Use the chart to interview several children for their responses.

   Examples:
   flowers, corn, vegetables, seeds
   shovel, seed, hoe, spade
   water, sunlight, dirt, fertilizer

2. Write their answers on word cards or pieces of sentences strips.
3. Model how to place the word cards over the blanks in the chart. Read the completed chart with the class.

   We see plants on our Earth.
   I will plant flowers.
   I will need a shovel.
   Plants need water.
   Plants need sunlight.

4. Repeat with additional words until the children can easily read the chart.
5. Place the interactive chart in the reading center, along with the word cards. Add any choices that might be necessary.
6. Students can complete the interactive chart during center time, using their information or their friends' information. Once the chart is complete, have students read the chart to someone in the center.
7. Give each child a copy of the "Plants" take-home book (see pattern on pages 165-166) and let him illustrate it.
8. Once a student completes his take-home book, have him read the book to a classmate.
9. Send the take-home books home with the students, and have students read the books to their parents, grandparents, siblings, etc.

Water

Preparation:
Make the "Water" chart using either lined chart paper or sentence strips and a pocket chart. Prepare several word cards or sentence strips for recording student responses.

Water
Our Earth is made of lots of water.
Water can be found in ____________________.
____________________ need water.
We use water to ____________________.
We need to take care of the water on our Earth.

Steps:

1. Introduce the blank interactive theme chart to students during "big group" time. Use the chart to interview several children for their responses.

   Examples:
   rivers, streams, oceans
   People, Plants, Animals
   drink, clean, take care of plants

2. Write their answers on word cards or pieces of sentence strips.
3. Model how to place the word cards over the blanks in the chart. Read the completed chart with the class.

   Our Earth is made of lots of water.
   Water can be found in rivers.
   People need water.
   We use water to drink.
   We need to take care of the water on our Earth.

4. Repeat with additional words/phrases until the children can easily read the chart.
5. Place the interactive chart in the reading center, along with the word cards. Add any choices that might be necessary.
6. Students can complete the interactive chart during center time, using their information or their friends' information. Once the chart is complete, have students read the chart to someone in the center.
7. Give each child a copy of the "Water" take-home book (see pattern on pages 169-170) and let her illustrate it.
8. Once a student completes her take-home book, have her read the book to a classmate.
9. Send the take-home books home with the students, and have students read the books to their parents, grandparents, siblings, etc.

Machines

Preparation:
Make the "Machines" chart using either lined chart paper or sentence strips and a pocket chart. Prepare several word cards or sentence strips for recording student responses.

Machines
Machines do work.
A ________________ is a machine.
It helps us ________________.
It is ________________.

Steps:

1. Introduce the blank interactive theme chart to students during "big group" time. Use the chart to interview several children for their responses.

   Examples:
   car, dishwasher, TV
   get places, clean dishes, watch shows
   big, small, shiny, pretty

2. Write their answers on word cards or pieces of sentence strips.
3. Model how to place the word cards over the blanks in the chart. Read the completed chart with the class.

   Machines do work.
   A car is a machine.
   It helps us get places.
   It is shiny.

4. Repeat with additional words/phrases until the children can easily read the chart.
5. Place the interactive chart in the reading center, along with the word cards. Add any choices that might be necessary.
6. Students can complete the interactive chart during center time, using their information or their friends' information. Once the chart is complete, have students read the chart to someone in the center.
7. Give each child a copy of the "Machines" take-home book (see pattern on pages 171-172) and let him illustrate it.
8. Once a student completes his take-home book, have him read the book to a classmate.
9. Send the take-home books home with the students, and have students read the books to their parents, grandparents, siblings, etc.

Transportation

Preparation:
Make the "Transportation" chart using either lined chart paper or sentence strips and a pocket chart. Prepare several word cards or sentence strips for recording student responses.

Transportation
A __________ is transportation.
It travels on __________.
It carries __________.
It is __________.

Steps:

1. Introduce the blank interactive theme chart to students during "big group" time. Use the chart to interview several children for their responses.

   Examples:
   car, train, boat
   roads, rails, water
   people, animals, stuff
   big, small, shiny, pretty

2. Write their answers on word cards or pieces of sentences strips.
3. Model how to place the word cards over the blanks in the chart. Read the completed chart with the class.

   A car is transportation.
   It travels on roads.
   It carries people.
   It is shiny.

4. Repeat with additional words until the children can easily read the chart.
5. Place the interactive chart in the reading center, along with the word cards. Add any choices that might be necessary.
6. Students can complete the interactive chart during center time, using their information or their friends' information. Once the chart is complete, have students read the chart to someone in the center.
7. Give each child a copy of the "Transportation" take-home book (see pattern on pages 173-176) and let her illustrate it.
8. Once a student completes her take-home book, have her read the book to a classmate.
9. Send the take-home books home with the students, and have students read the books to their parents, grandparents, siblings, etc.

______ be quick.

______ be quick.

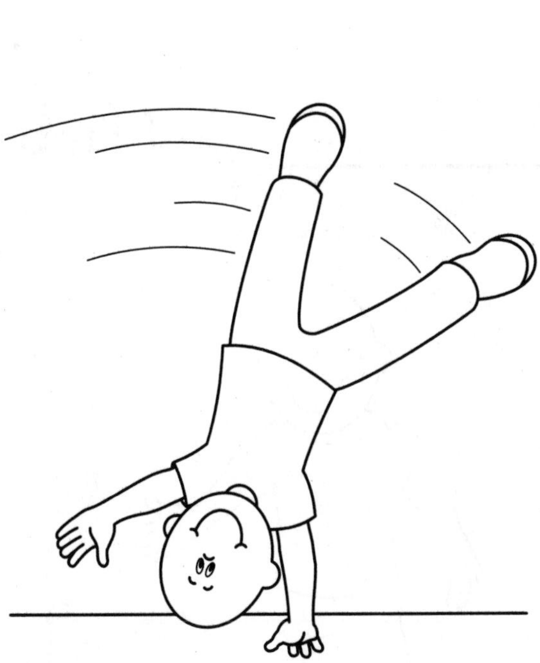

______ be nimble,

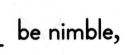

______ jump over the candlestick.

jump ________ over the candlestick.

3

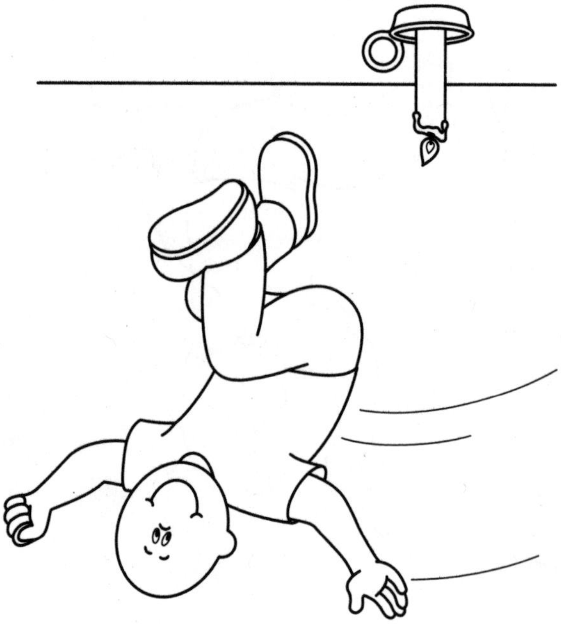

________ be nimble,

4

________ Be Nimble

Written, illustrated, and read by

____

Come again another day;

2

Come again another day;

5

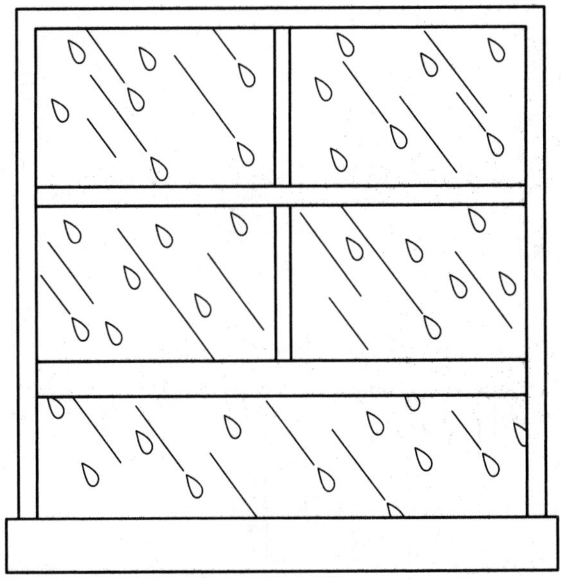

Rain, rain, go away,

1

Little ______________________

wants to play.

6

Rain, rain, go away,

4

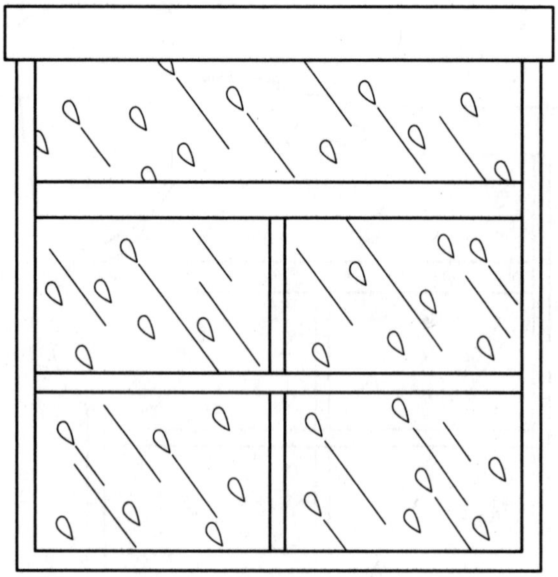

Little ________ wants to play.

3

Written, illustrated, and read by

____

Rain

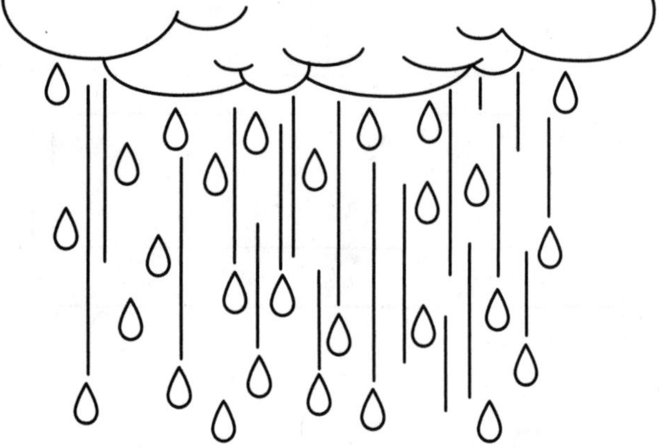

_______ stole the cookie from the cookie jar.

2

Not I.

5

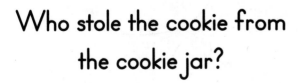

Who stole the cookie from the cookie jar?

1

Then, who?

6

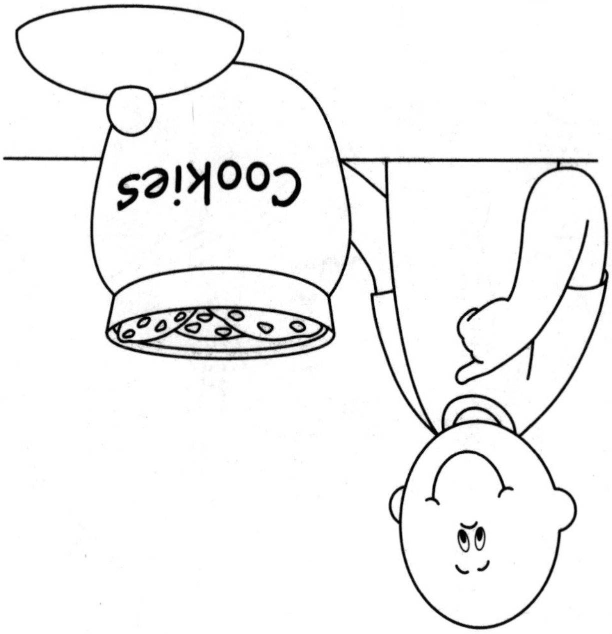

Who, me?

3

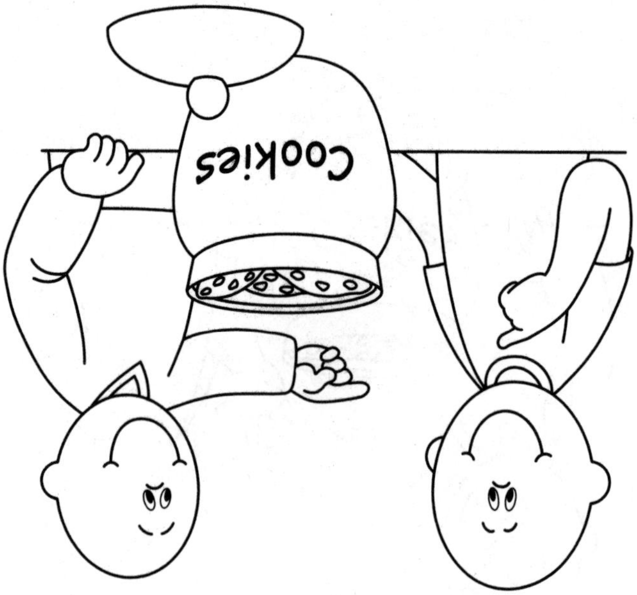

Yes, you!

4

Written, illustrated, and read by

____

Cookie Jar

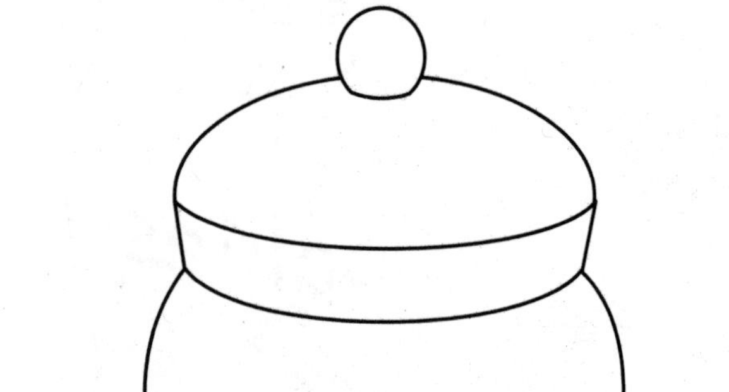

_________, put the kettle on.

1

_________, put the kettle on.
_________, put the kettle on.

2

_________, take it off again.
_________, take it off again.

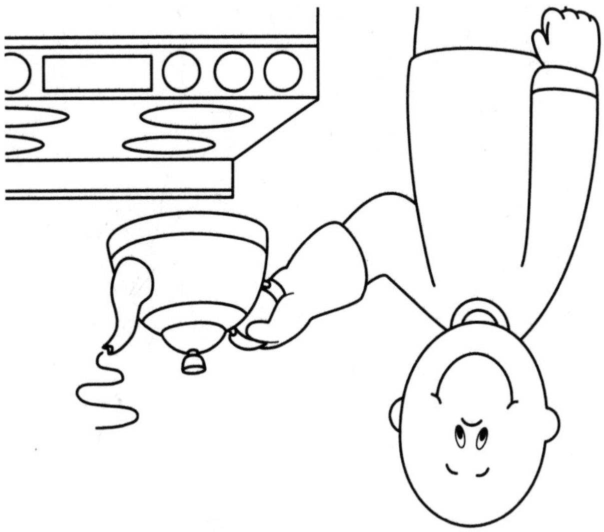

5

They've all gone away.

6

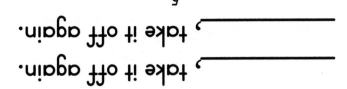

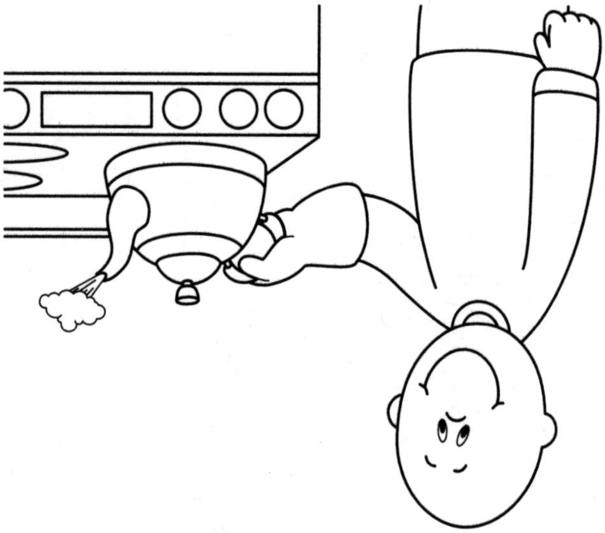

______, take it off again.

4

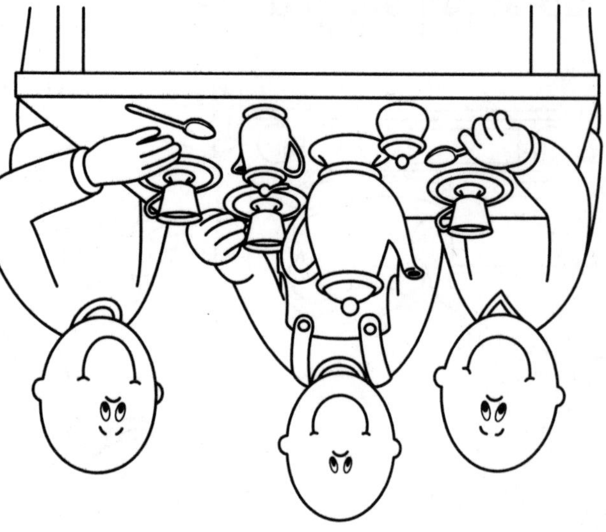

We'll all have tea.

3

______ and ______

Written, illustrated, and read by

____

My ________ name is
________________.

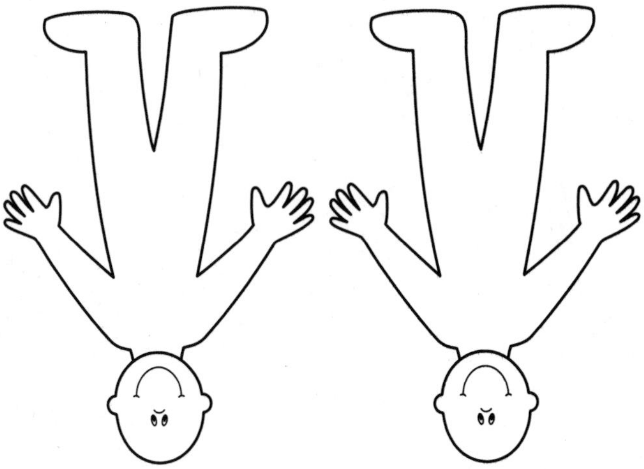

2

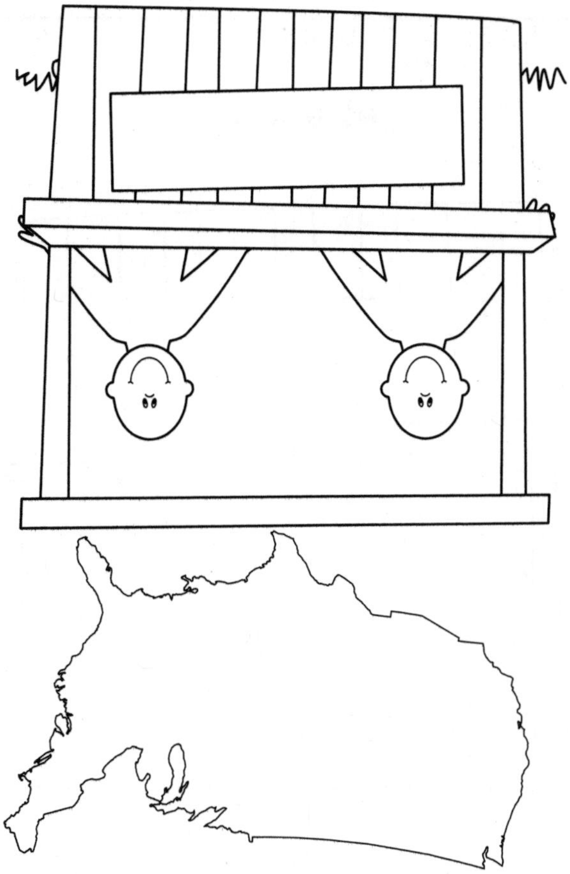

5

________, my name
is ____________________.

1

Written, illustrated, and read
by

____

6

We come from

________.

3

And we sell

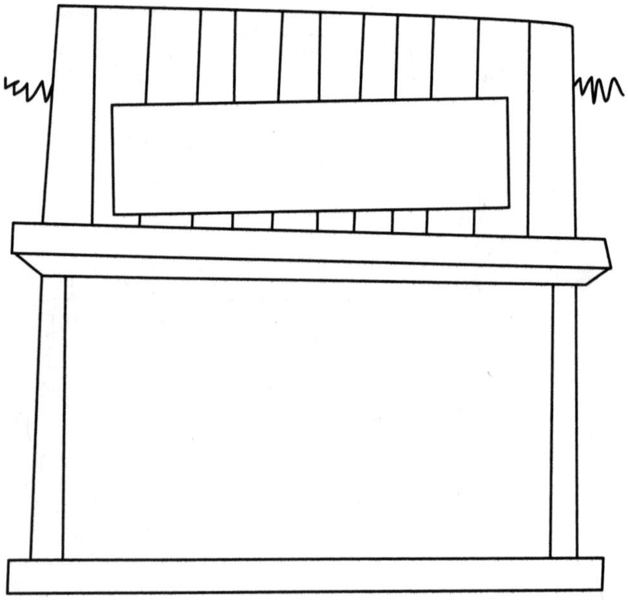

________.

4

____, My Name Is

____

This book was published by a member of

____

Class

Five little ducks went out to play,

Over the hills and far away.

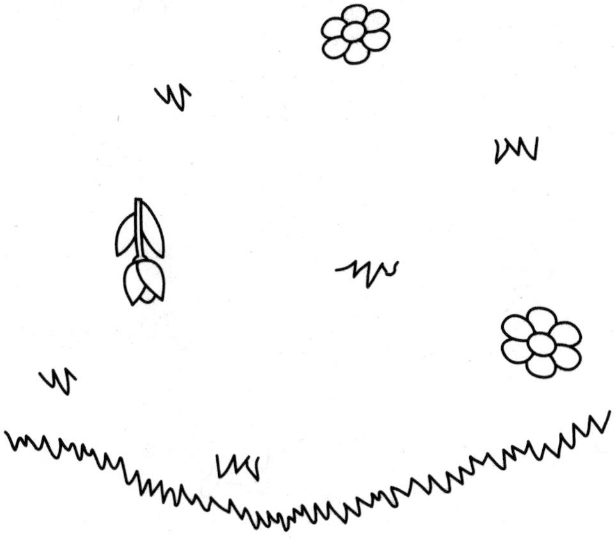

No little ducks went out to play,
over the hills and far away.

Mama Duck said,
"QUACK, QUACK, QUACK."
Five little ducks came running back.

Mama Duck said,
"Quack, quack, quack."
No little ducks came running back.

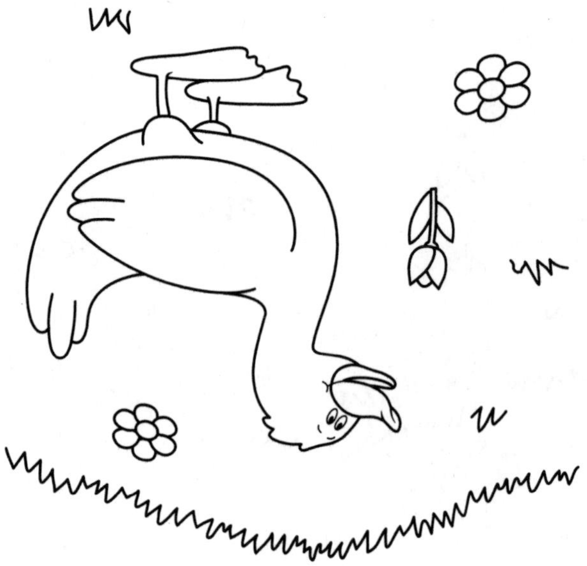

12

Mama Duck said,
"Quack, quack, quack."

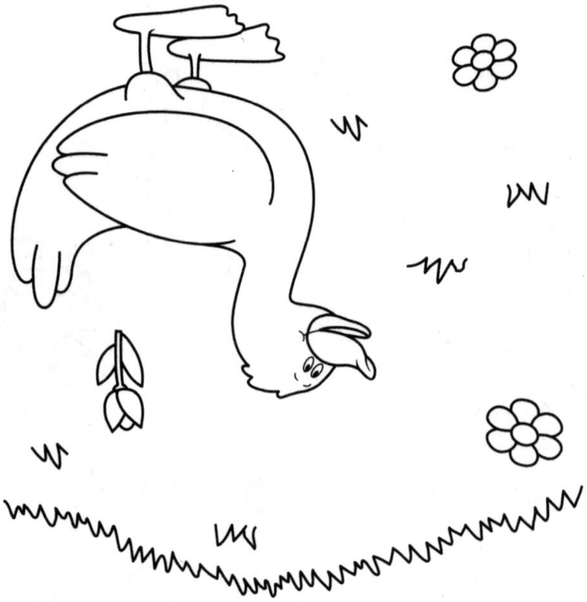

3

Illustrated and read
by

____

Five Little Ducks

Mama Duck said,
"Quack, quack, quack."
Three little ducks came running back.

9

Two little ducks went out to play,
over the hills and far away.

6

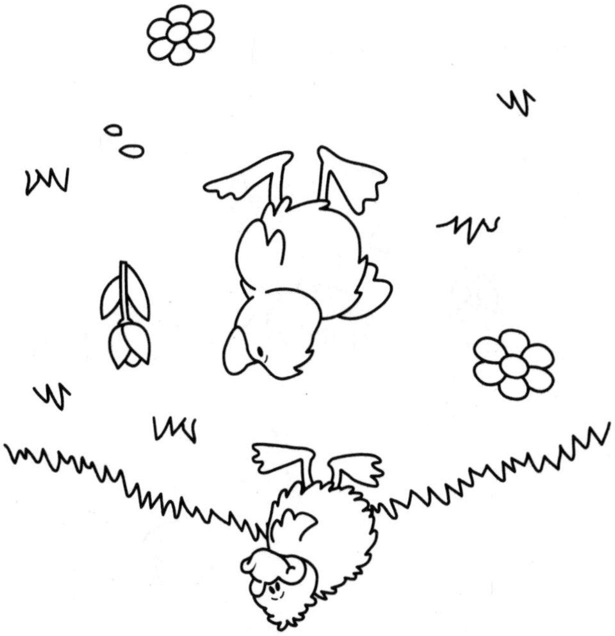

Four little ducks went out to play,
over the hills and far away.

5

Mama Duck said,
"Quack, quack, quack."
One little duck came running back.

10

Mama Duck said,
"Quack, quack, quack."
Two little ducks came running back.

Three little ducks went out to play,
over the hills and far away.

One little duck went out to play,
over the hills and far away.

Four little ducks
came running back.

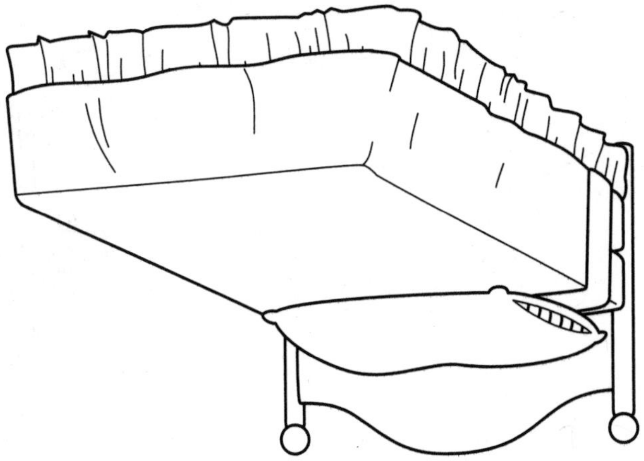

"Roll over.

10

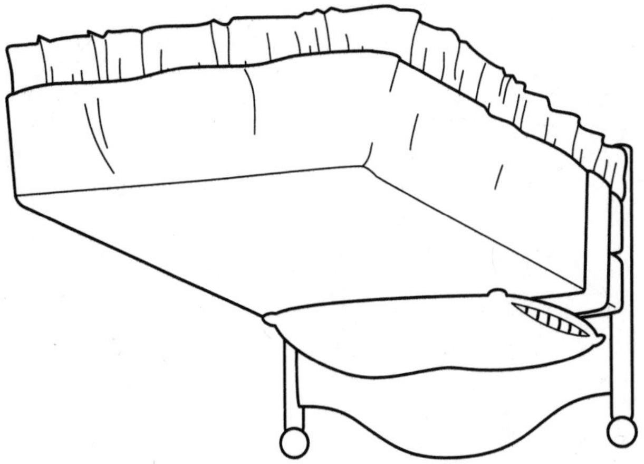

There were three in the bed
And the little one said,

13

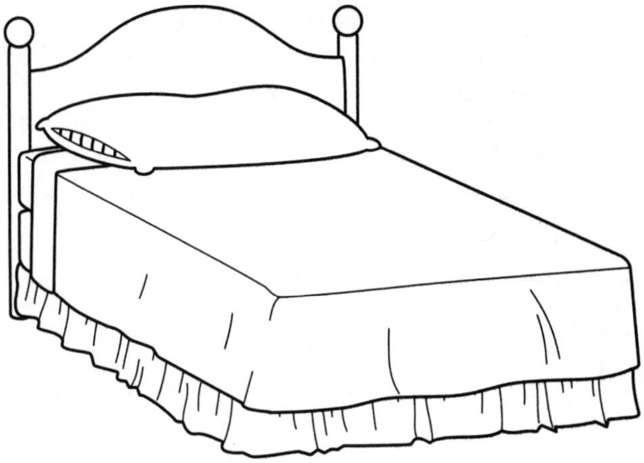

There were six in the bed
And the little one said,

1

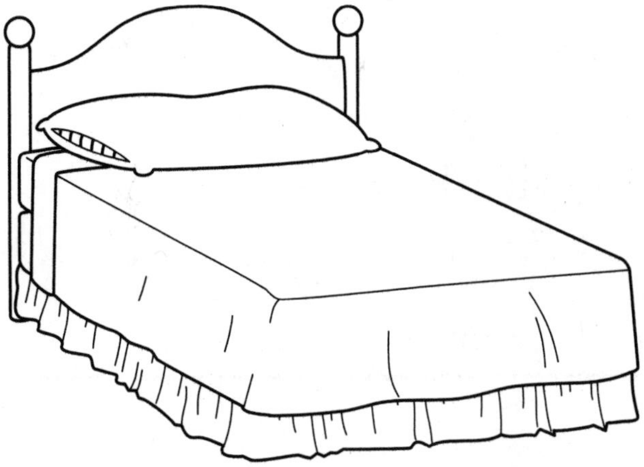

"Good night."

22

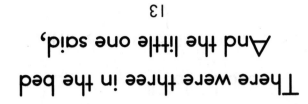

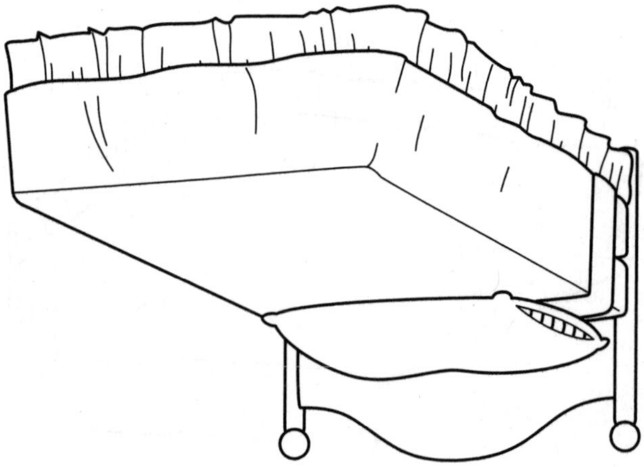

Roll over."

11

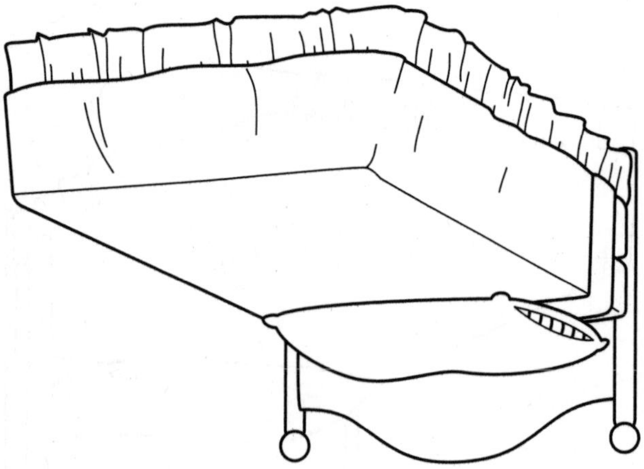

So they all rolled over
And one fell out.

12

Six in the Bed

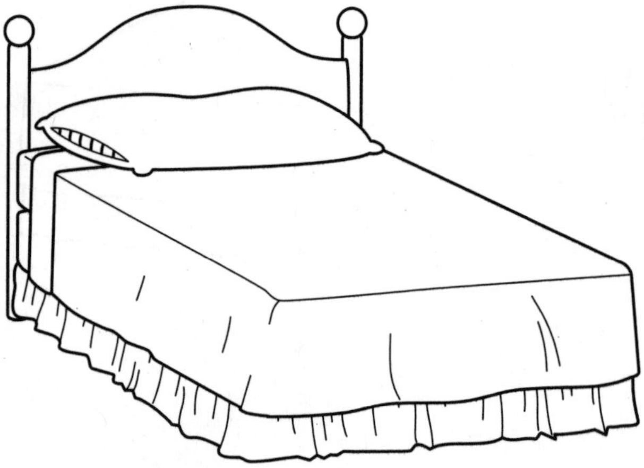

Illustrated and read
by

____

So they all rolled over
And one fell out.

8

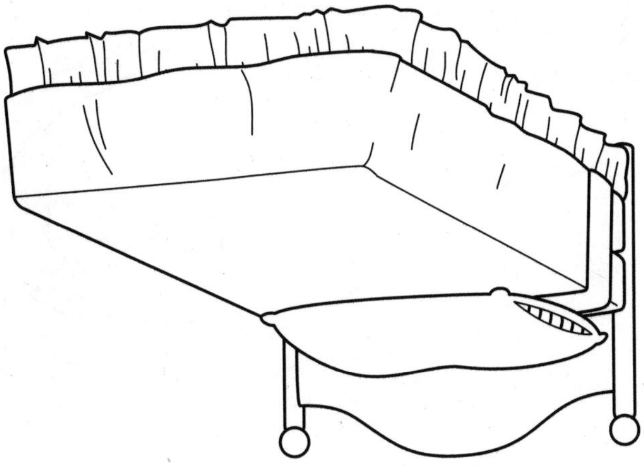

Roll over.”

15

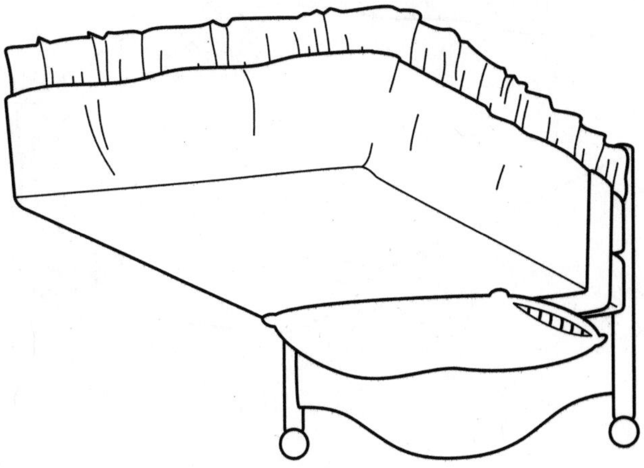

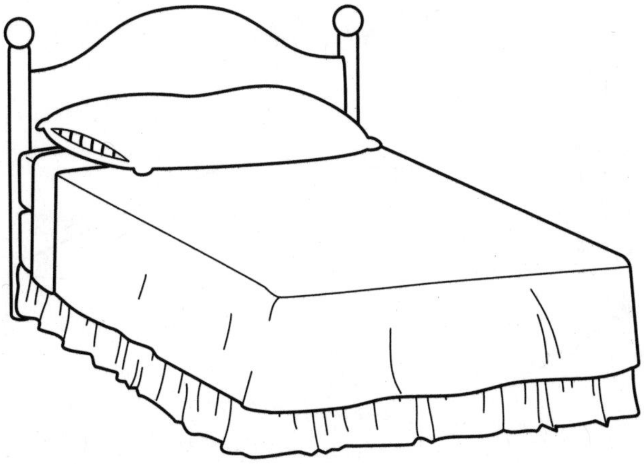

Roll over.”

3

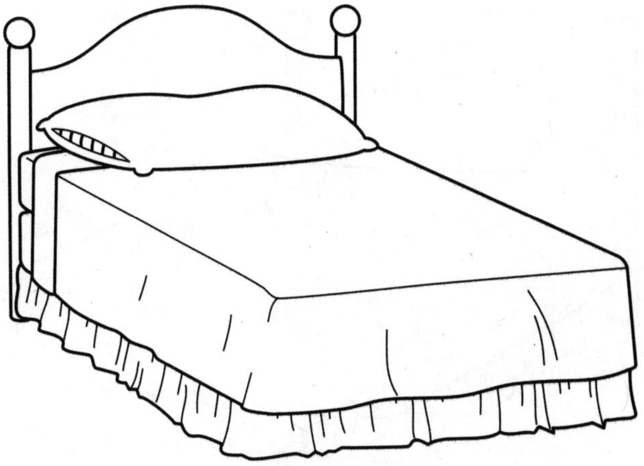

So they all rolled over
And one fell out.

20

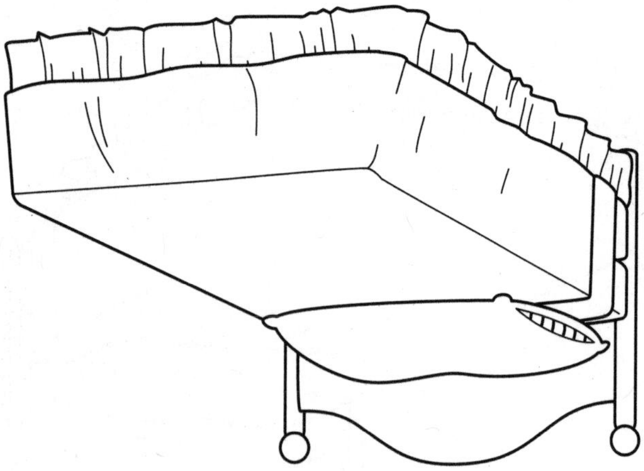

"Roll over.

14

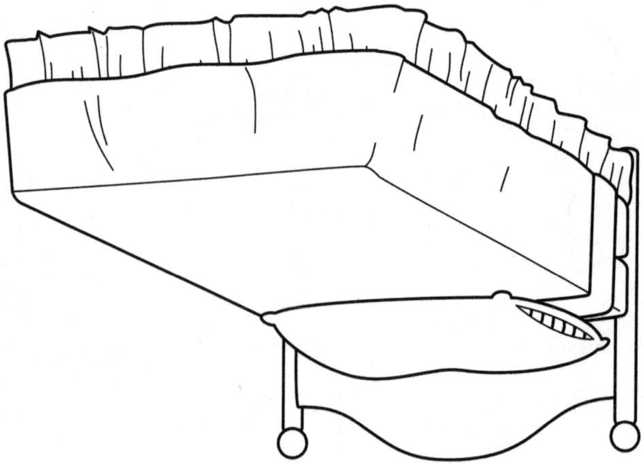

There were four in the bed
And the little one said,

6

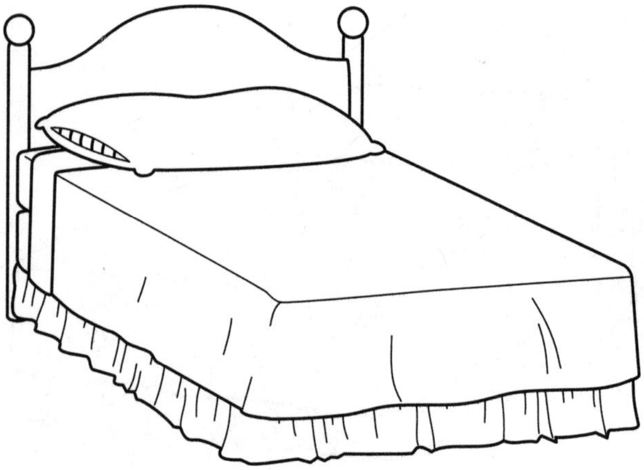

There was one in the bed
And the little one said,

21

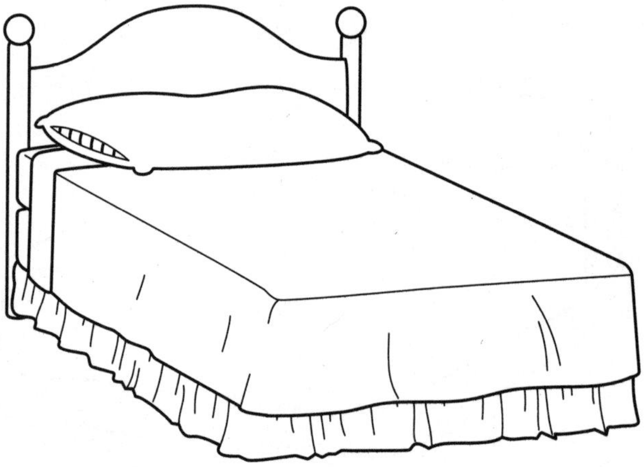

"Roll over.

2

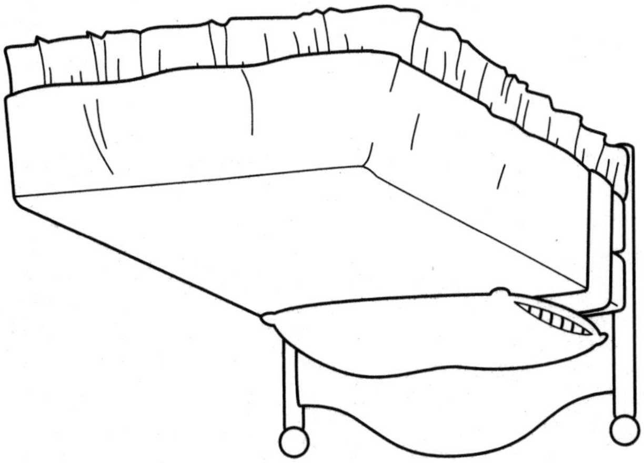

“Roll over.

9

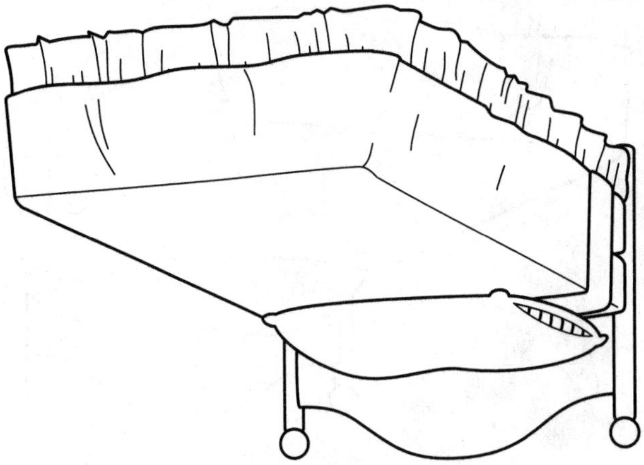

There were two in the bed
And the little one said,

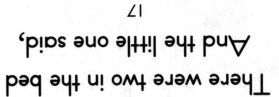

17

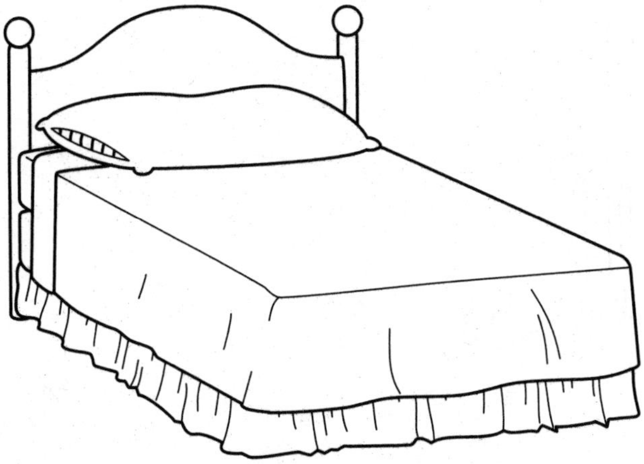

There were five in the bed
And the little one said,

5

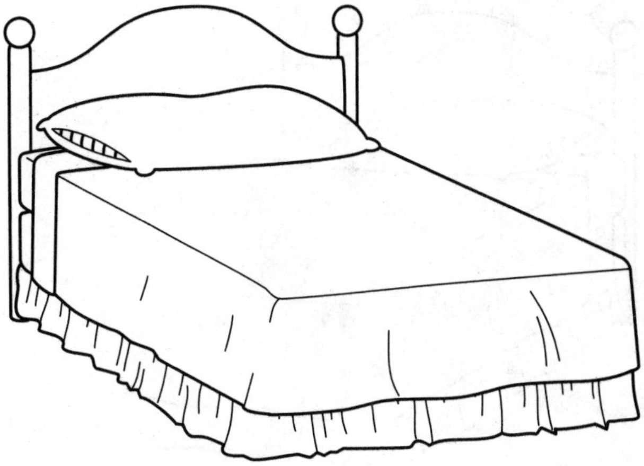

“Roll over.

18

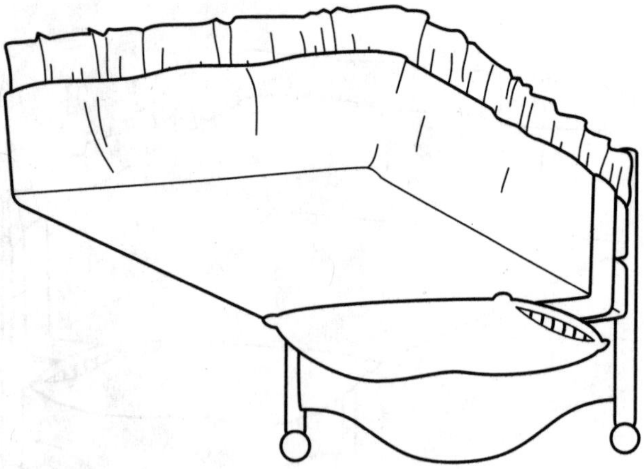

So they all rolled over
And one fell out.

16

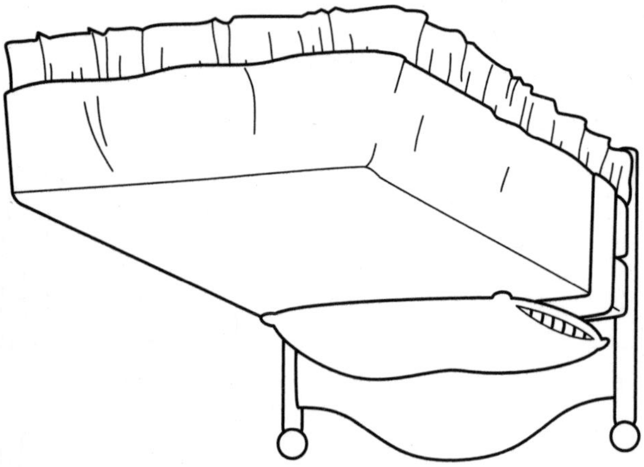

Roll over."

7

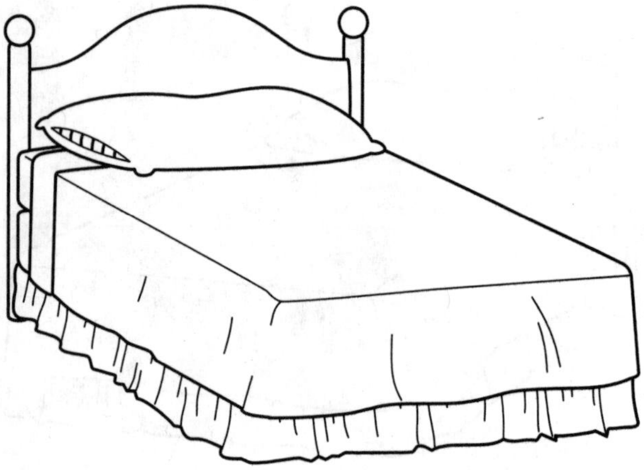

Roll over."

19

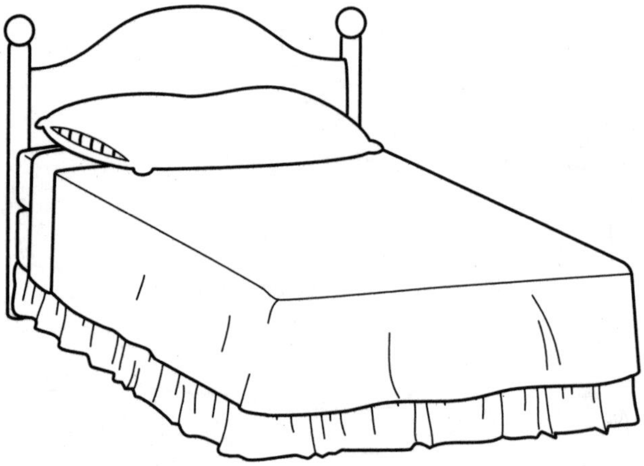

So they all rolled over
And one fell out.

4

2

And if one green bottle
should accidentally fall,

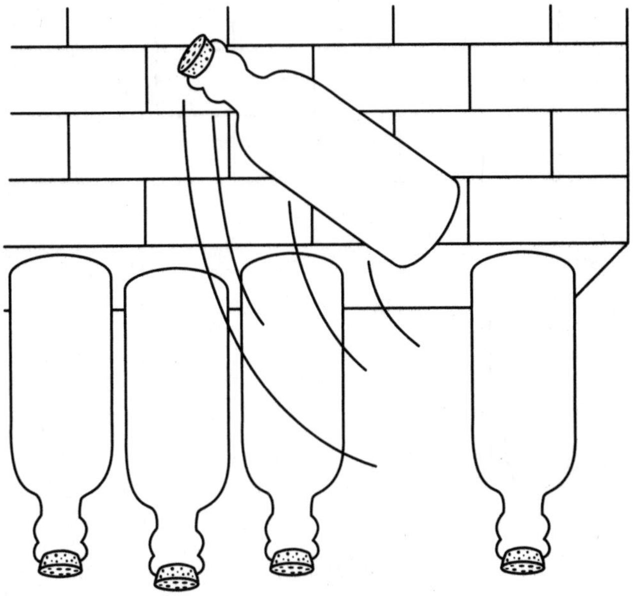

13

One green bottle
sitting on the wall,
One green bottle
sitting on the wall,

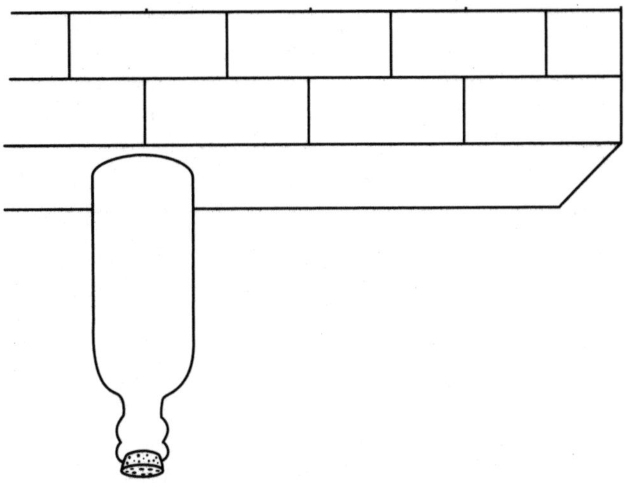

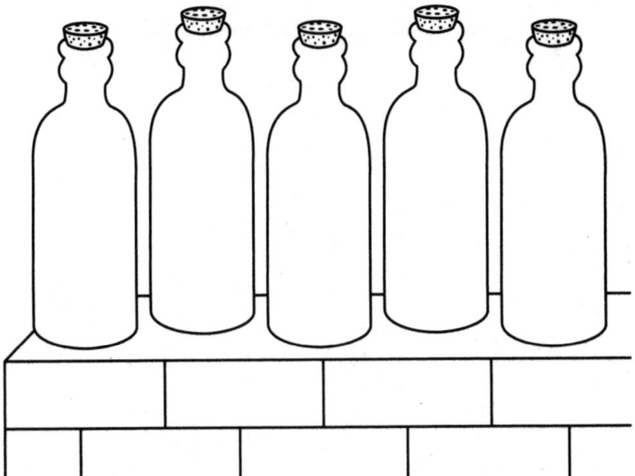

Five green bottles
sitting on the wall,
Five green bottles
sitting on the wall,

1

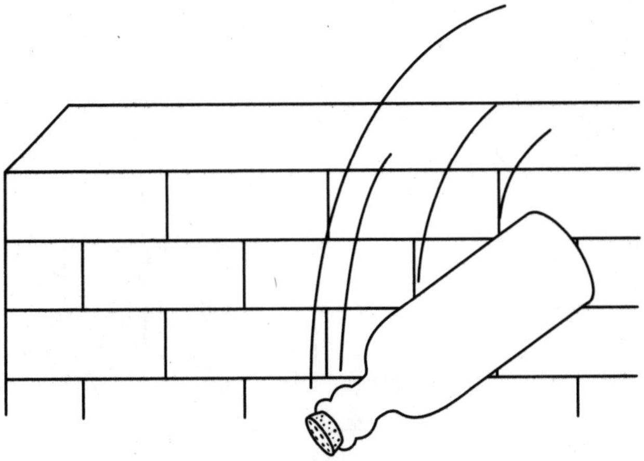

And if one green bottle
should accidentally fall,

14

There'd be one green bottle
sitting on the wall.

12

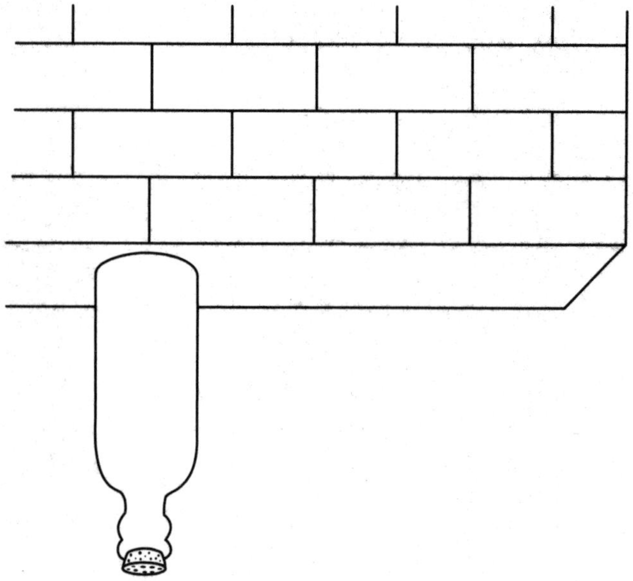

There'd be four green bottles
sitting on the wall.

3

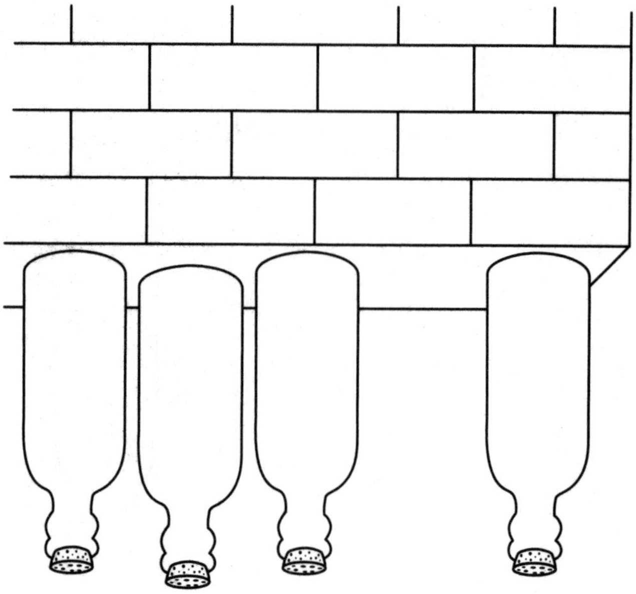

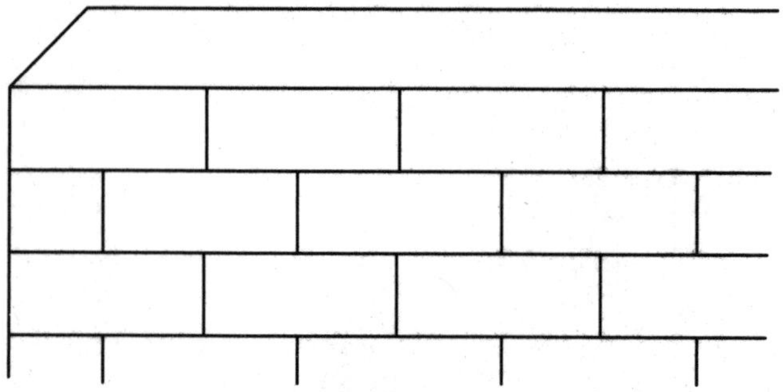

No green bottles
sitting on the wall.

Five Green Bottles

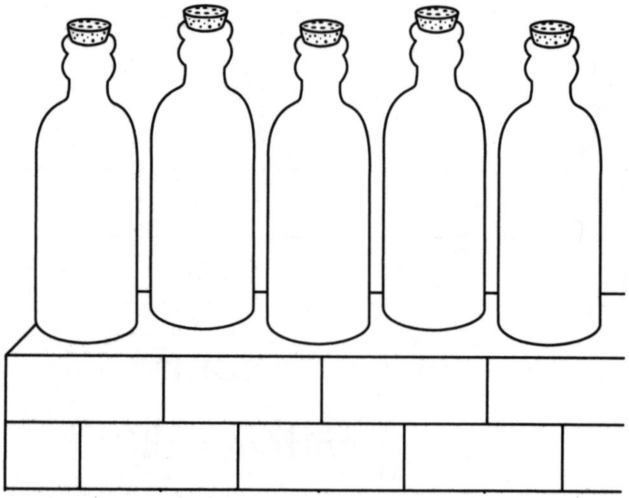

by

____

6

There'd be three green bottles
sitting on the wall.

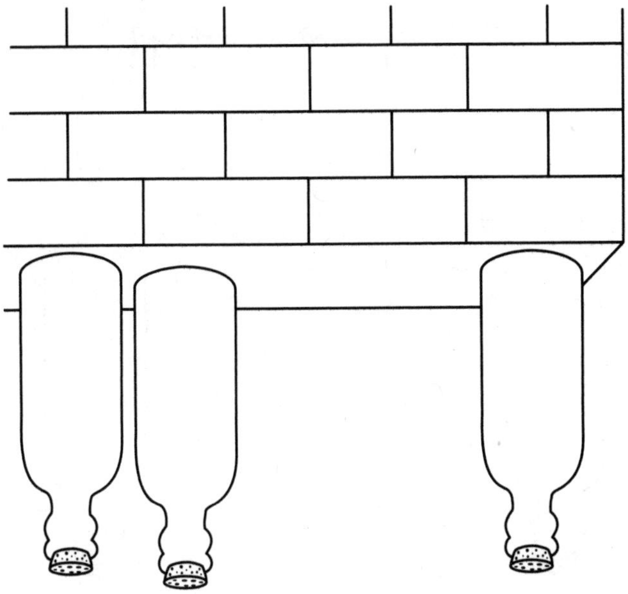

9

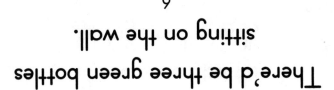

There'd be two green bottles
sitting on the wall.

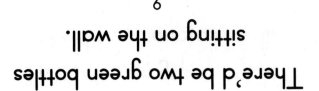

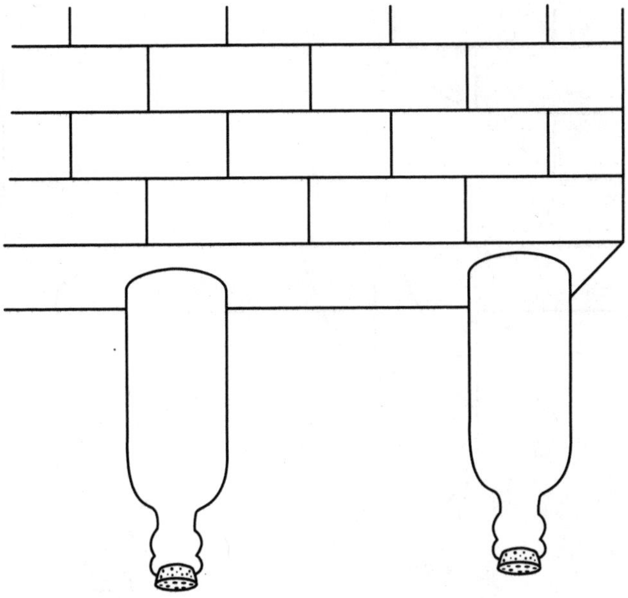

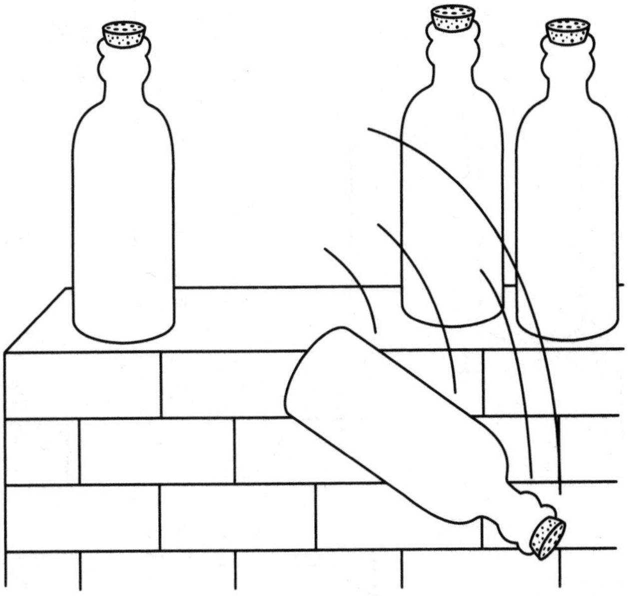

and if one green bottle
should accidentally fall,

5

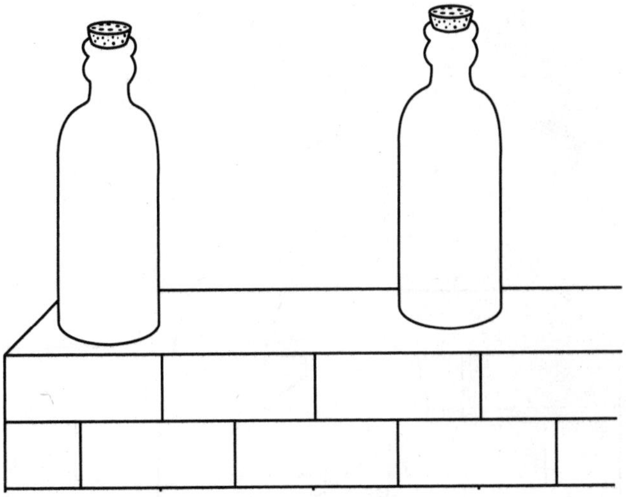

Two green bottles
sitting on the wall,
Two green bottles
sitting on the wall,

10

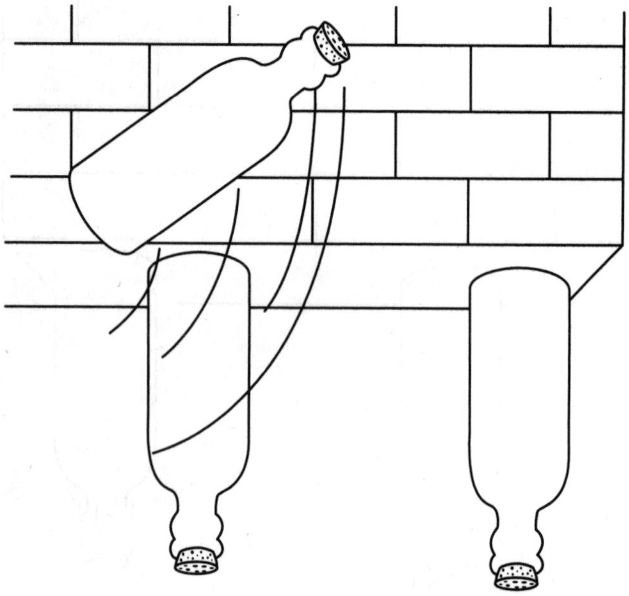

And if one green bottle
should accidentally fall,

8

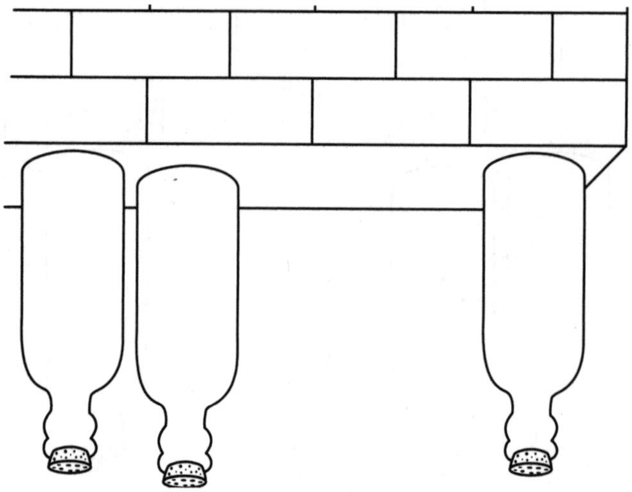

Three green bottles
sitting on the wall,
Three green bottles
sitting on the wall,

7

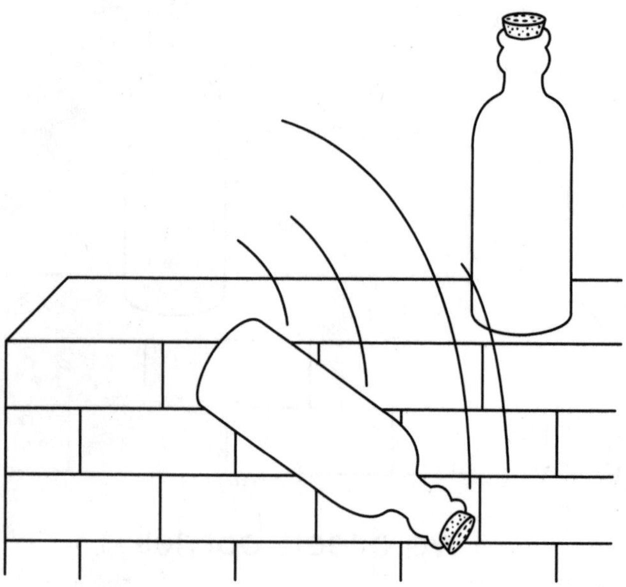

And if one green bottle
should accidentally fall,

11

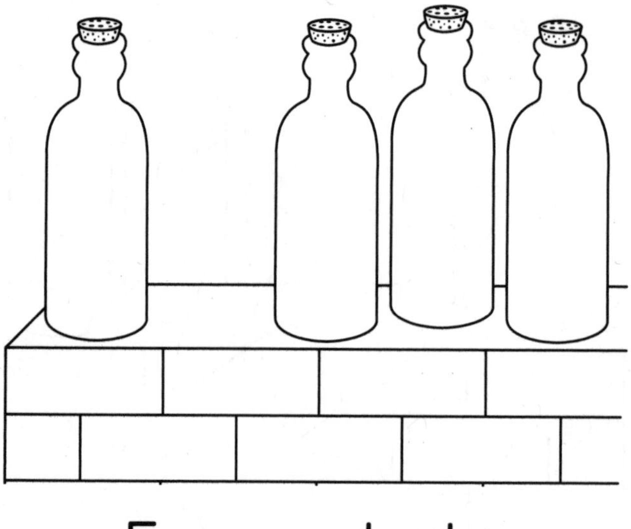

Four green bottles
sitting on the wall,
Four green bottles
sitting on the wall,

4

This old man,
He played one,

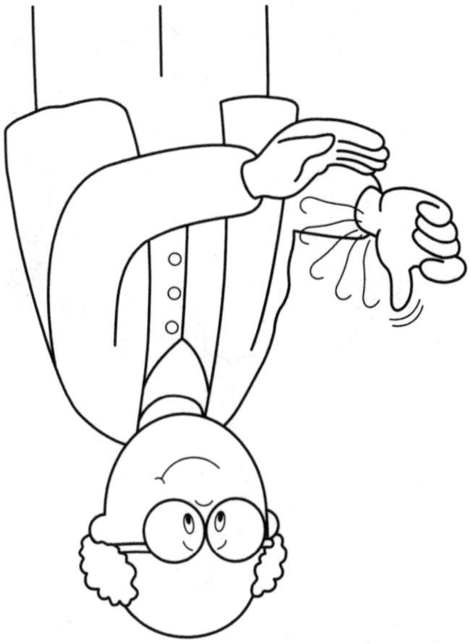

He played knick knack
with his thumb.
With a knick knack, paddy whack,

This old man,
He played five,

He played knick knack
on a hive.
With a knick knack, paddy whack,

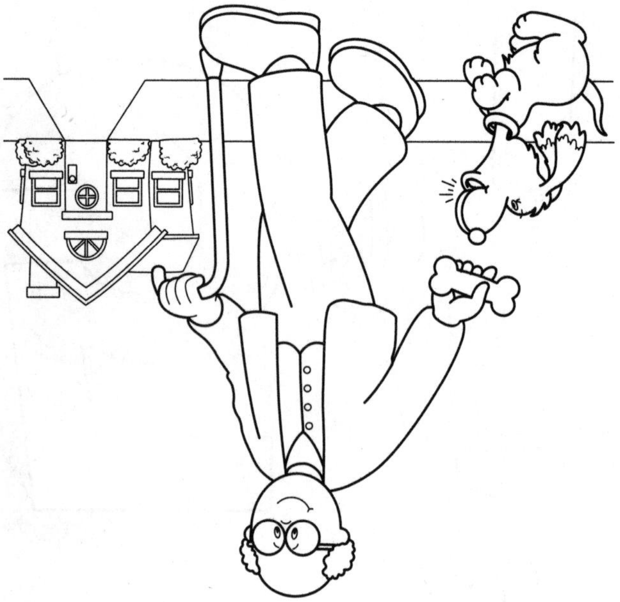

Give a dog a bone,
This old man came rolling home.

12

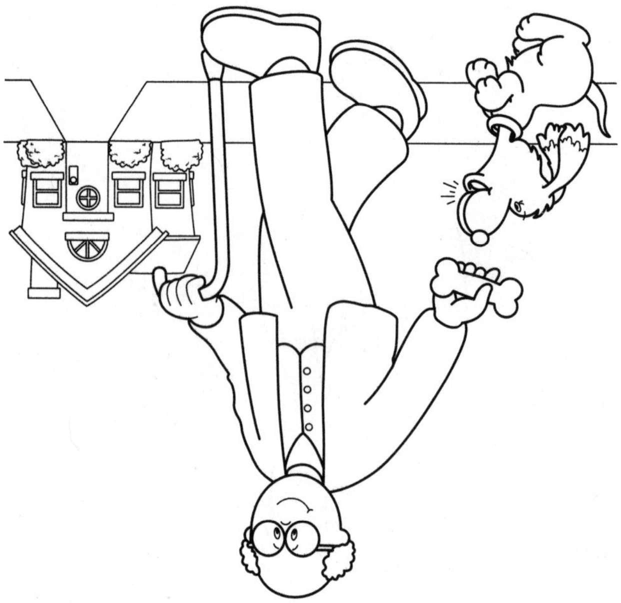

Give a dog a bone,
This old man came rolling home.

3

90

Give a dog a bone,
This old man came rolling home.

This Old Man

by

____

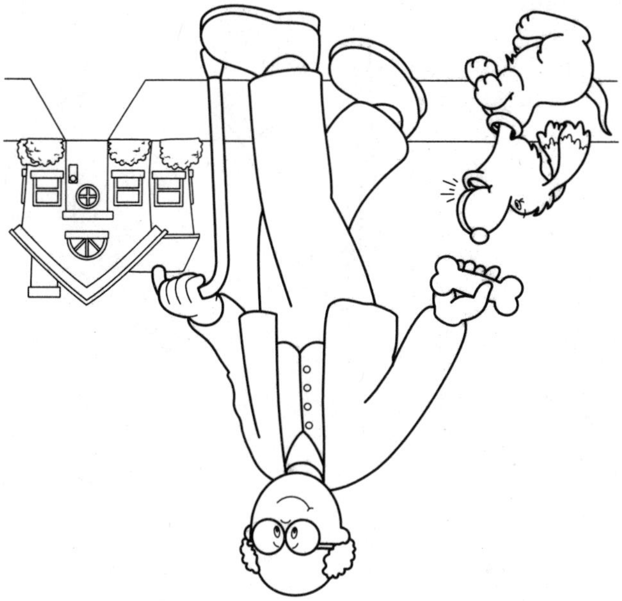

Give a dog a bone,
This old man came rolling home.

9

Give a dog a bone,
This old man came rolling home.

9

He played knick knack
on my shoe.
With a knick knack, paddy whack,

5

This old man,
He played four,

10

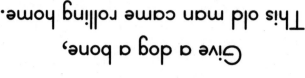

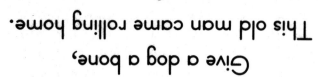

He played knick knack
on my knee.
With a knick knack, paddy whack,

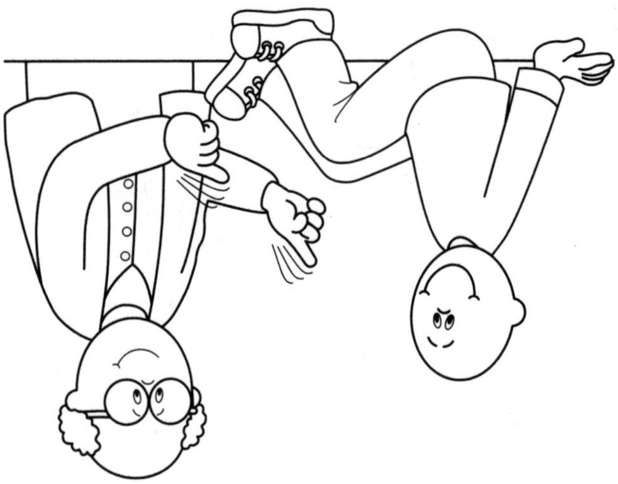

8

This old man,
He played three,

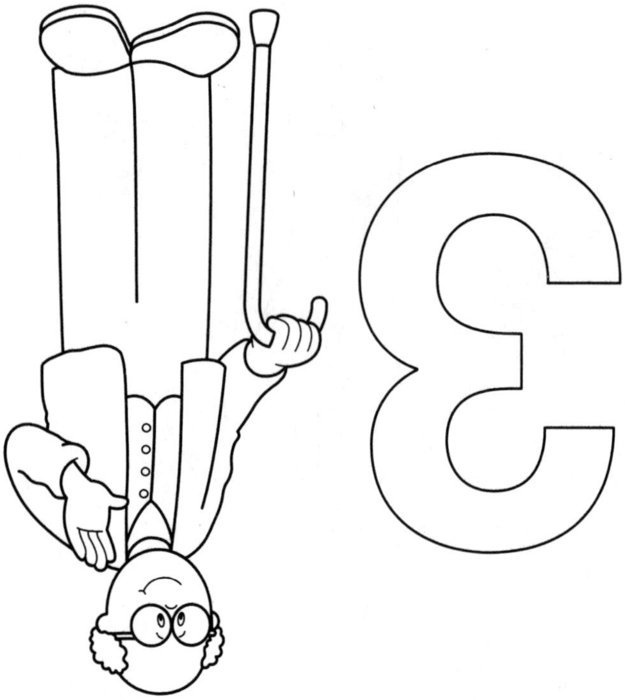

7

He played knick knack
at my door.
With a knick knack, paddy whack,

11

This old man,
He played two,

4

In a ____________ pot.

2

5

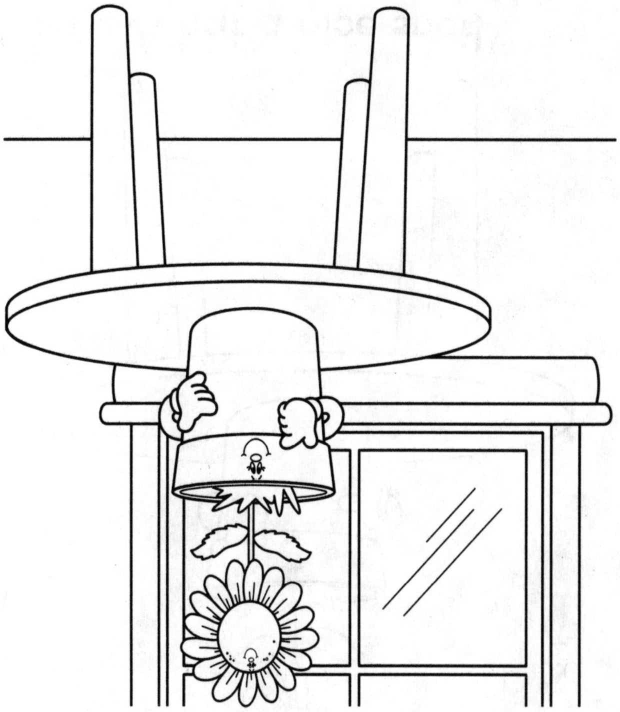

Pretty little flower

1

Illustrated and read
by

____

6

The Flowerpot

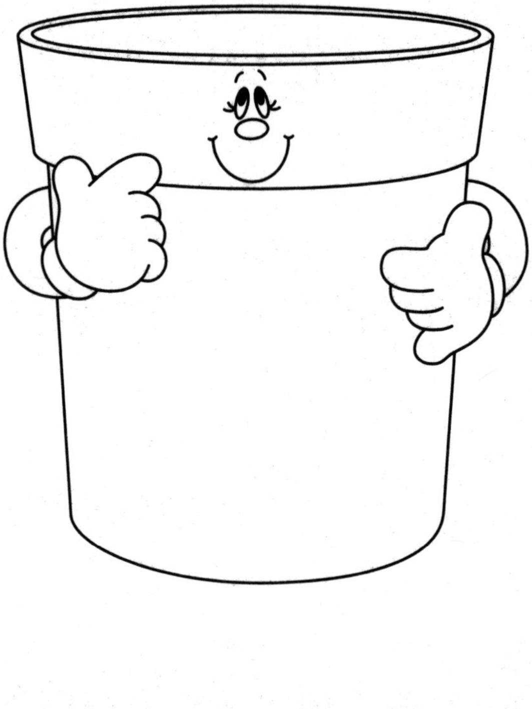

Published by a member of

____

Class

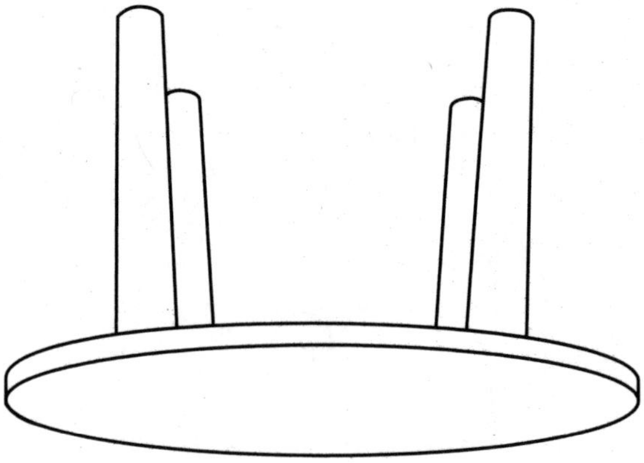

Put it on a table.

3

What a nice spot!

4

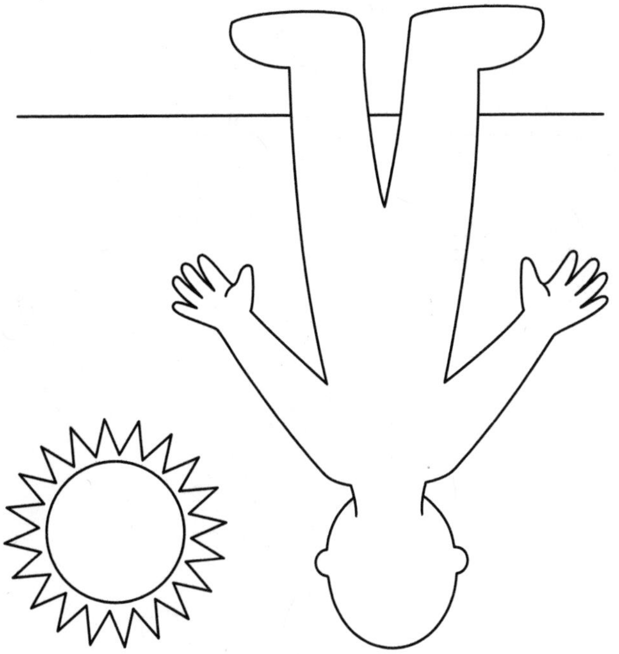

2

5

________________ wore a

____________ ______________,

1

____________ wore a

_____________ _______________

all day long.

6

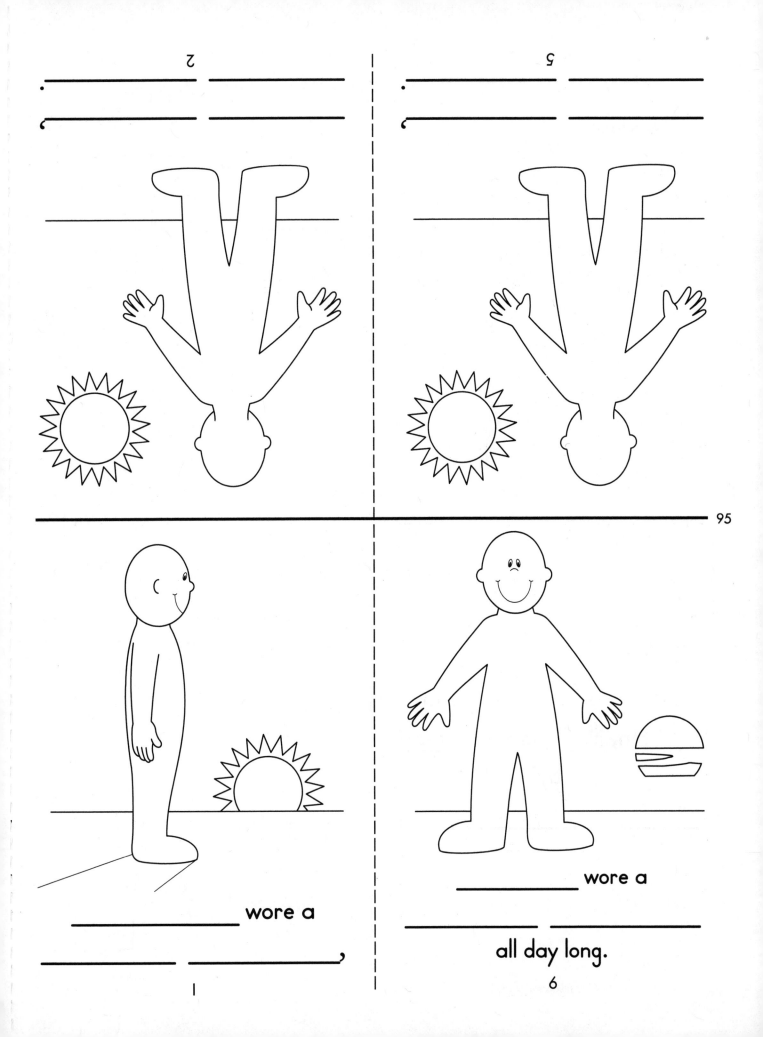

_______ wore a
_______ _______ all day long.

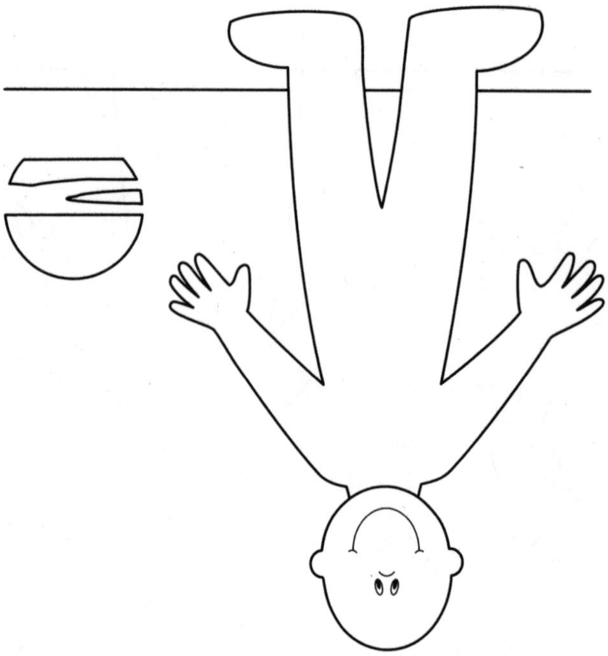

3

_______ wore a
_______ _______?

4

96

_______ Wore a
_______ _______

Written, illustrated, and read by

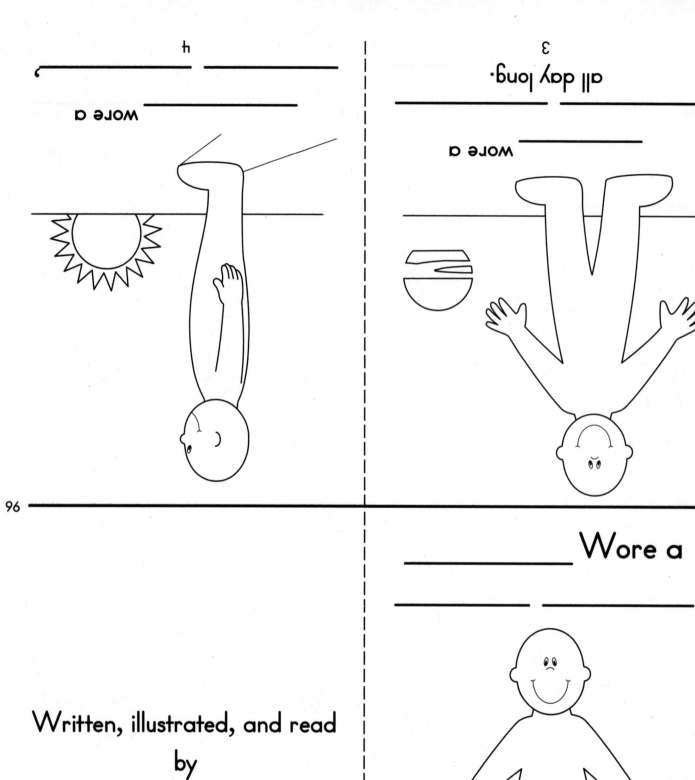

____

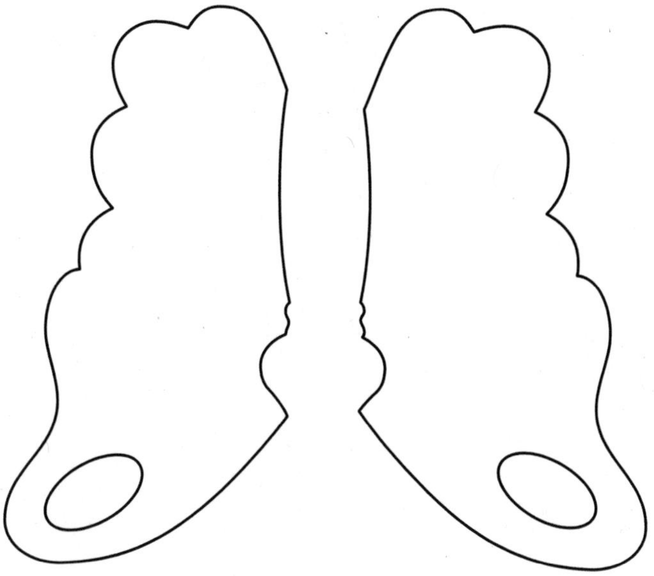

With a little yellow spot,

2

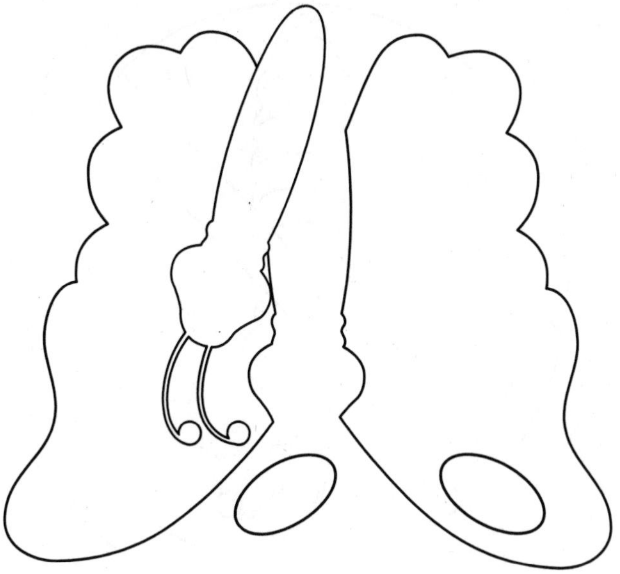

What is it?

5

Shiny green wings

1

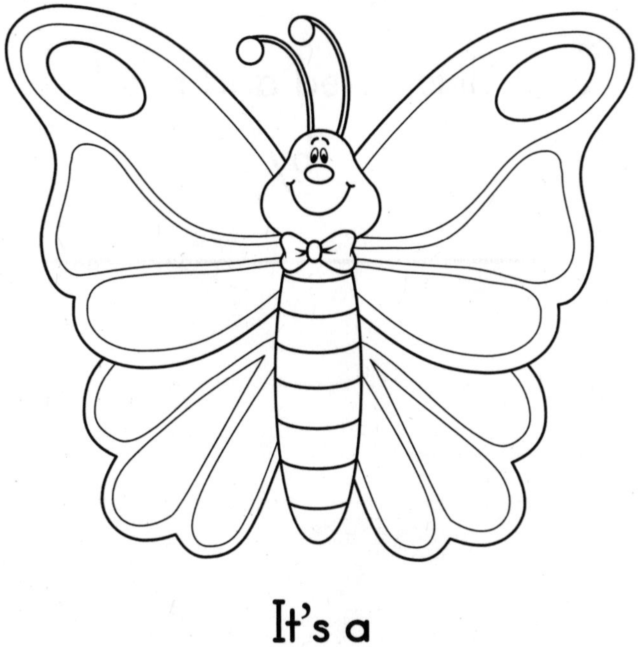

It's a

______________________.

6

A caterpillar it's not.

4

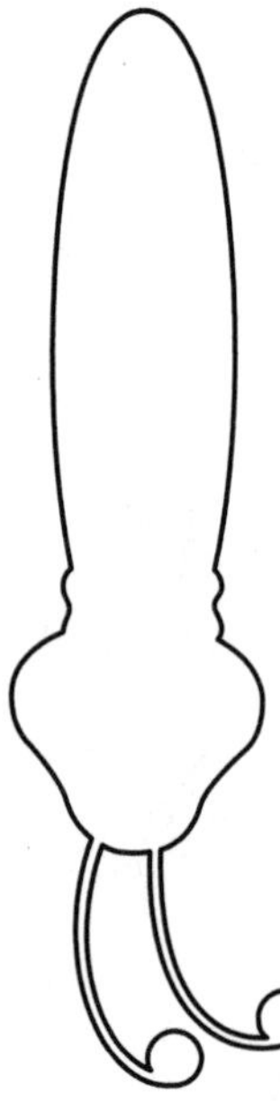

Fuzzy brown body,

3

Illustrated and read

by

____

What Is It?

Then, the red one.

2

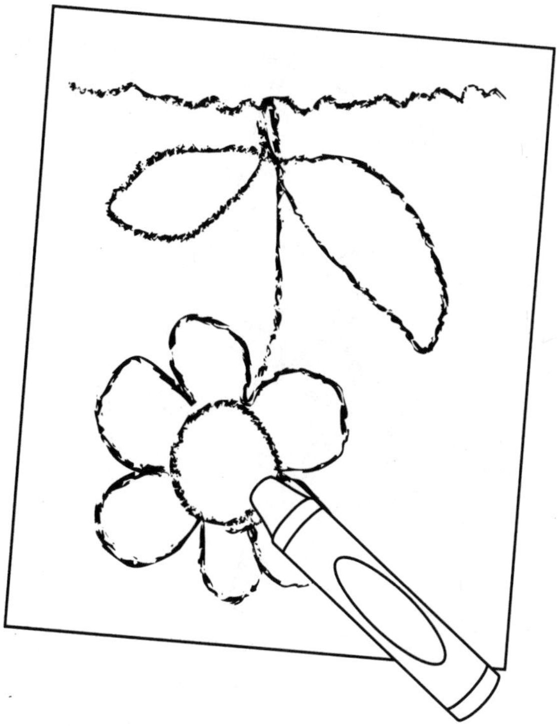

Color the crayons.

5

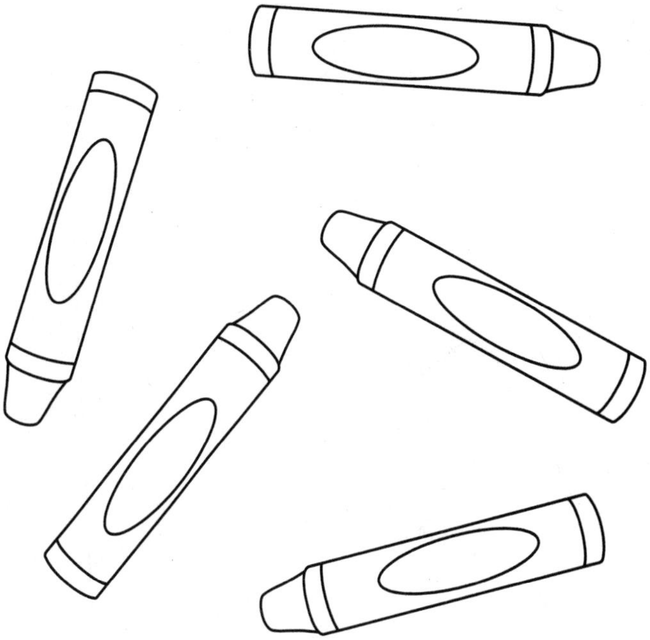

First use the blue,

1

Illustrated and read
by

____

6

Put them all away

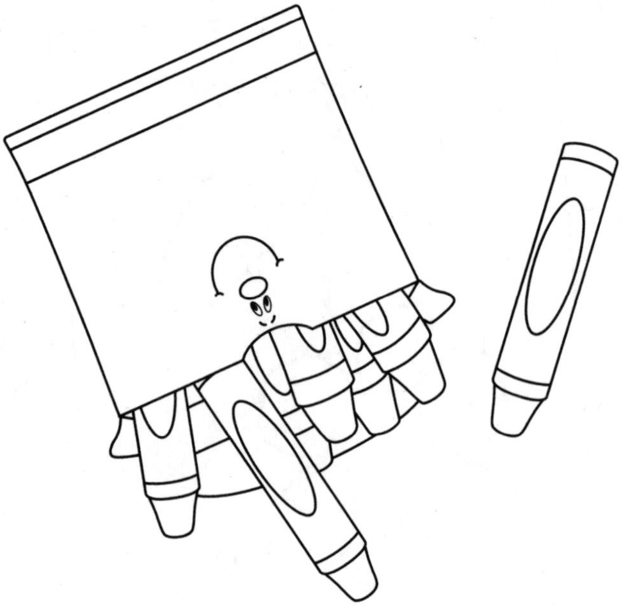

3

When you are done.

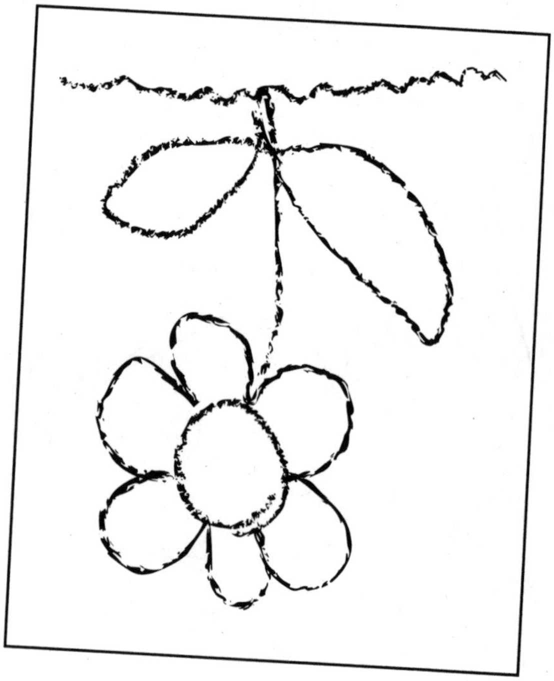

4

Crayons

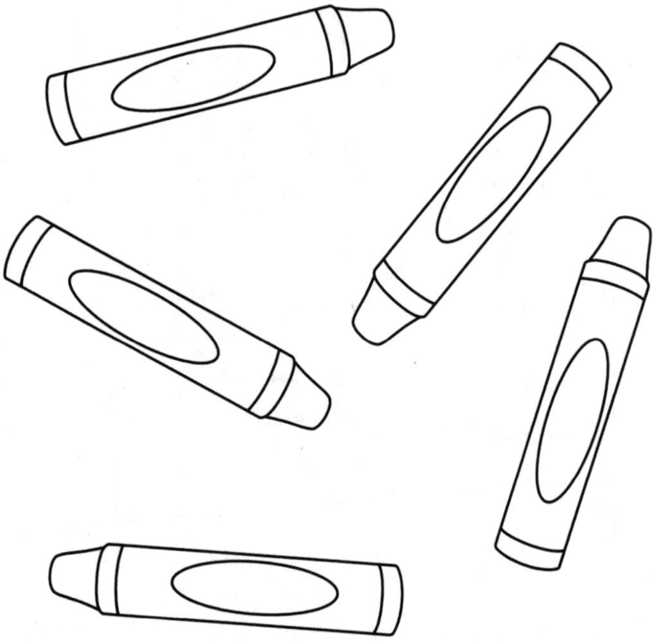

Published by a member of

____

Class

turn around.

2

Teddy Bear, Teddy Bear,

13

Teddy Bear, Teddy Bear,

1

turn out the lights.

14

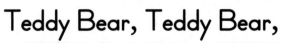

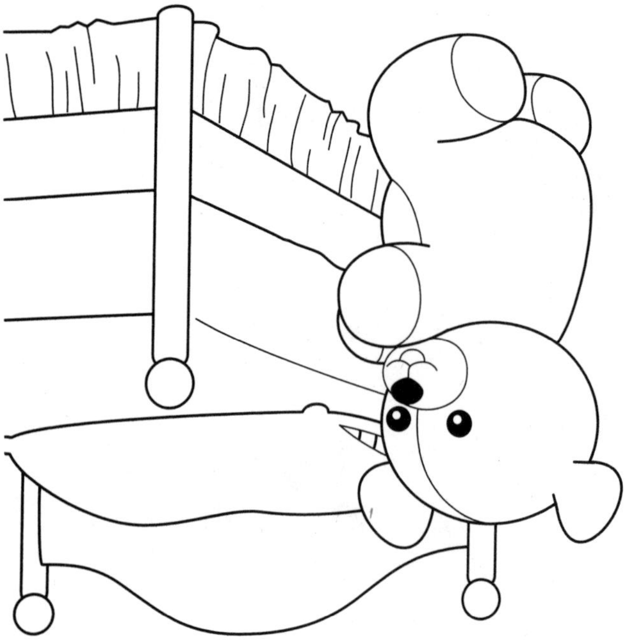

say your prayers.

12

Teddy Bear, Teddy Bear,

3

Teddy Bear, Teddy Bear,

say, "Good night!"

Teddy Bear, Teddy Bear

by

____

show your shoe.

Teddy Bear, Teddy Bear,

Teddy Bear, Teddy Bear,

go upstairs.

Teddy Bear, Teddy Bear,

7

that will do!

8

Teddy Bear, Teddy Bear,

11

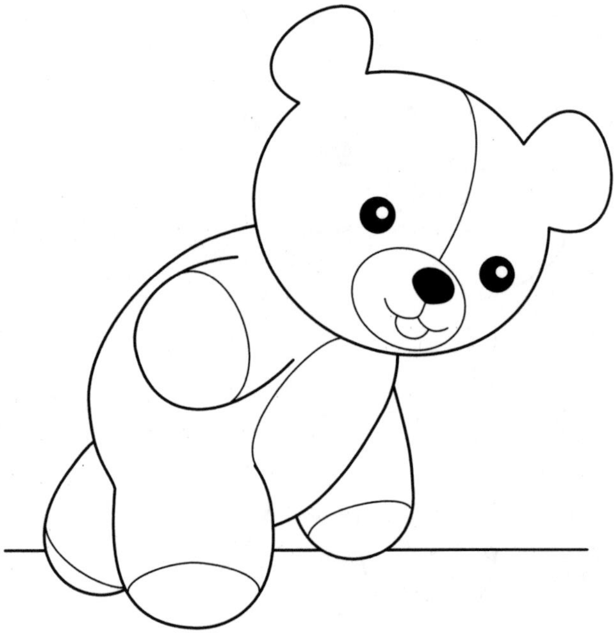

touch the ground.

4

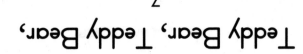

A–hunting we will go.

2

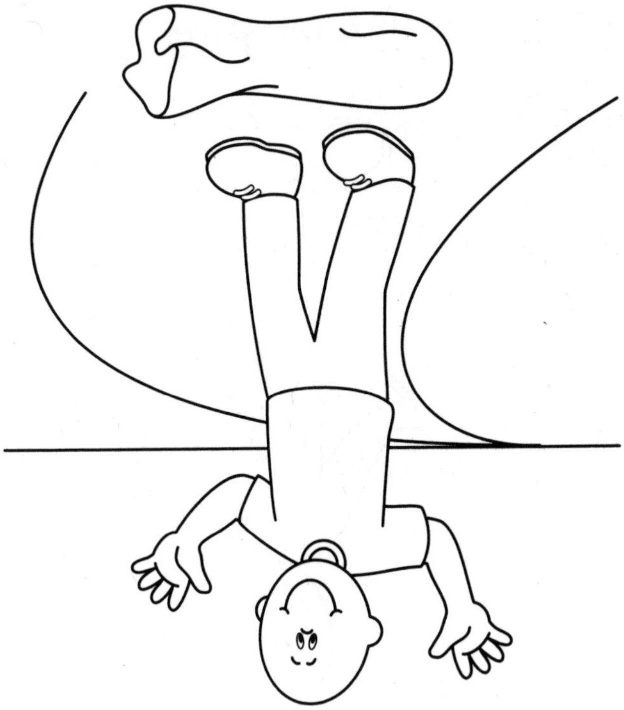

And then we'll let it go.

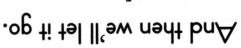

5

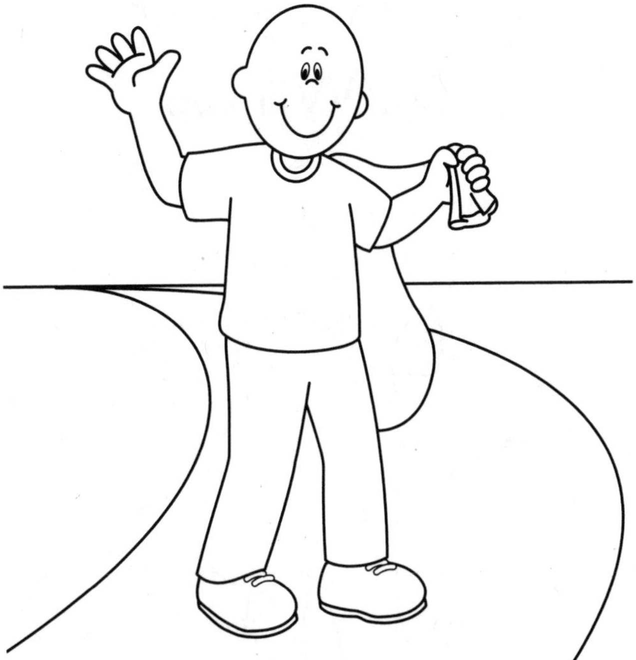

Oh, a–hunting we will go,

1

Written, illustrated, and read by

____

6

4

And put it in a

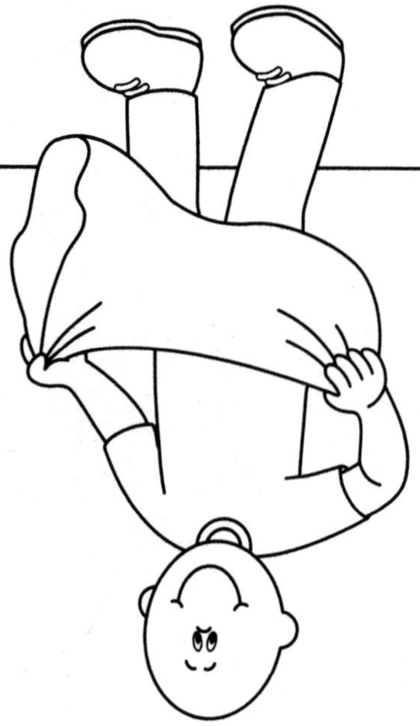

3

We'll catch a

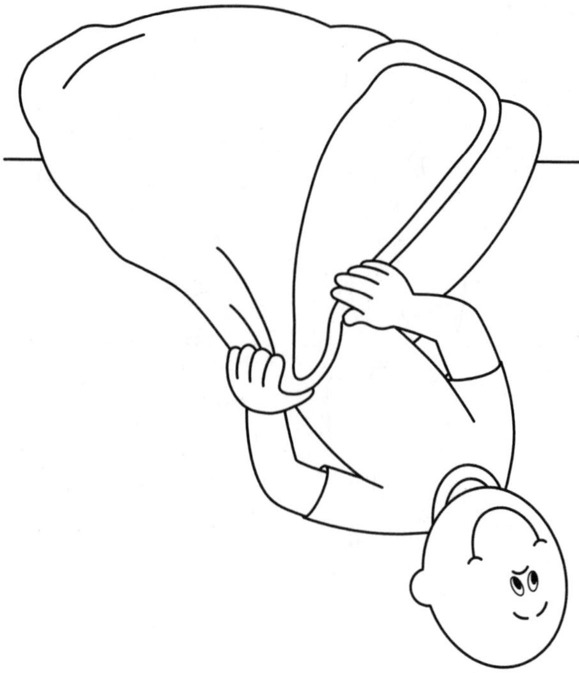

Published by a member of

Class

Oh, A-Hunting We Will Go

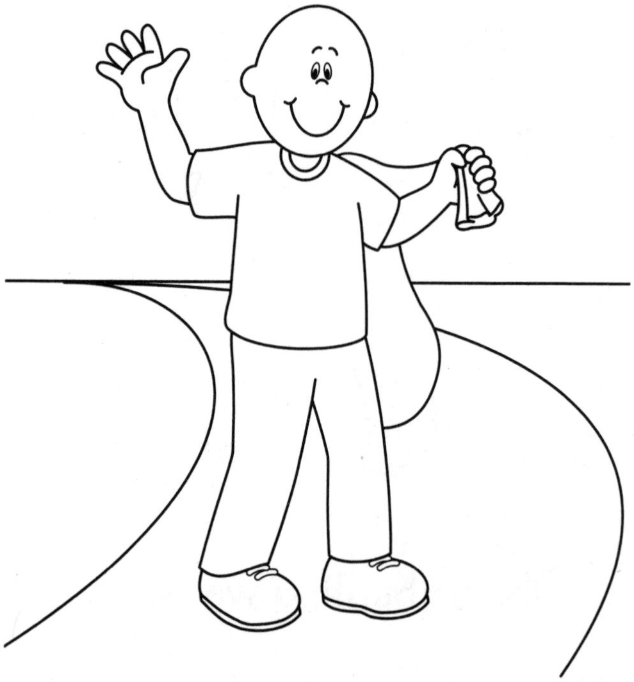

2

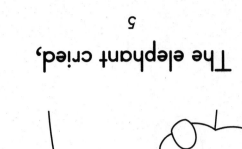

Where the corncobs grow,

5

The elephant cried,

Down in the meadow,

1

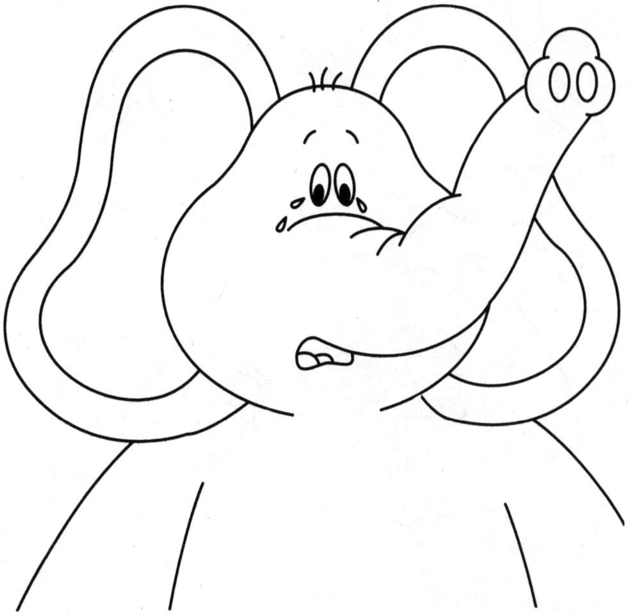

With tears in his eyes,

6

4

On an elephant's toe.

3

A grasshopper jumped

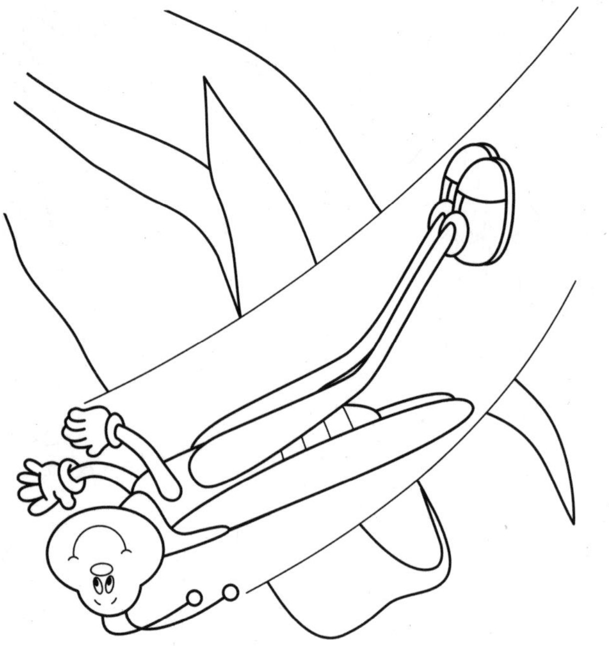

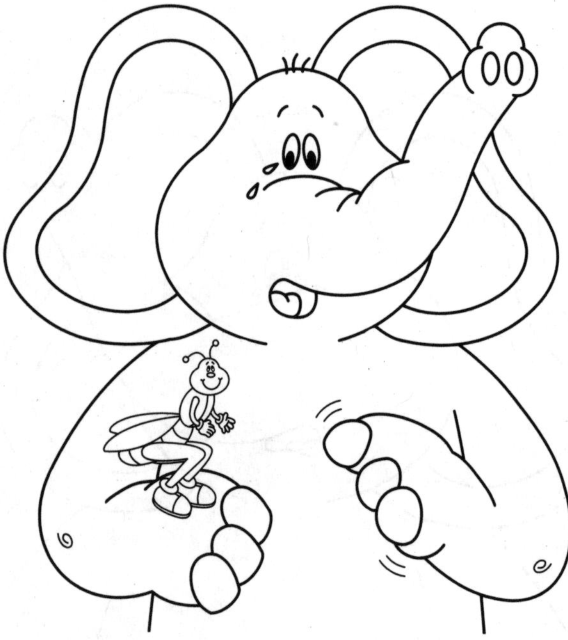

"Why don't you pick on
Someone your own size?"

Down in the Meadow

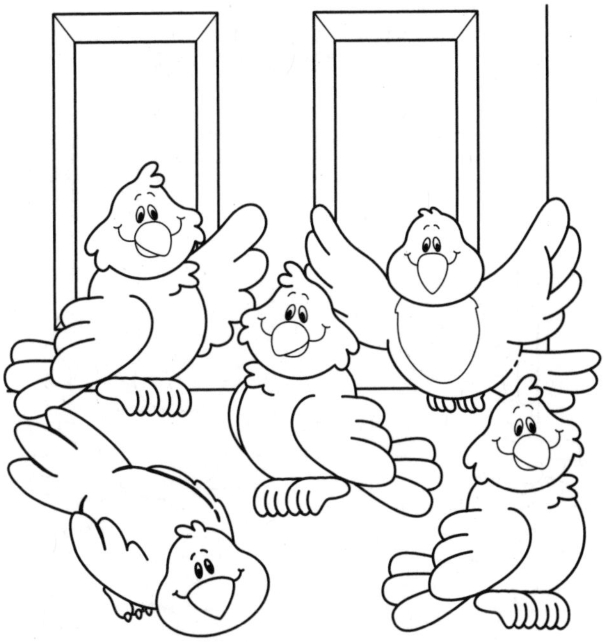

Five little chickadees,
sitting by the door.

One flew away,

One little chickadee,
sitting all alone.

That one flew away,

and then there was one.

12

and then there were four.

3

and then there were none.

Chickadees

by

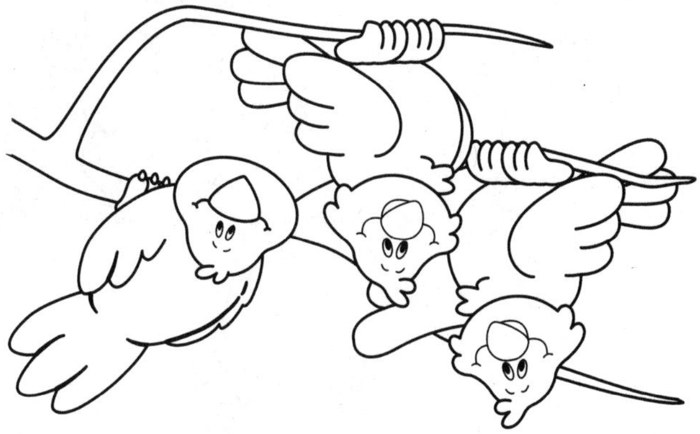

and then there were three.

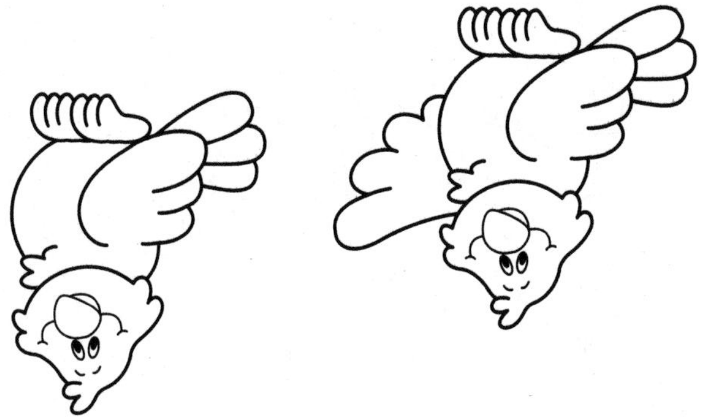

and then there were two.

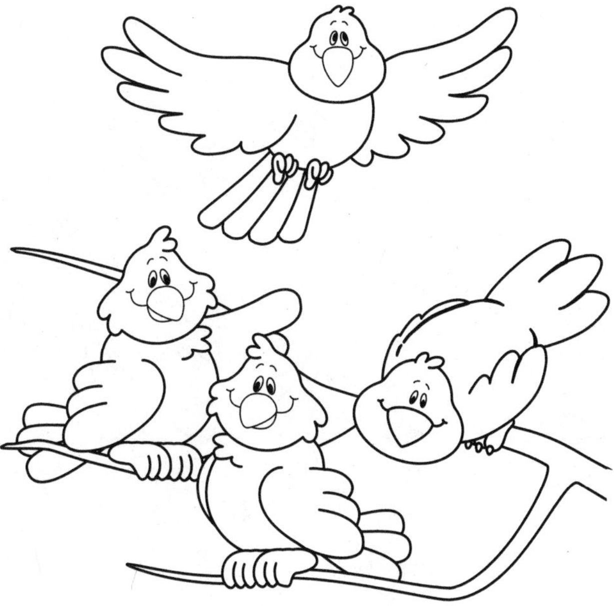

One flew away,

Two little chickadees,
sitting in the sun.

One flew away,

Three little chickadees,
looking at you.

One flew away,

Four little chickadees,
sitting in a tree.

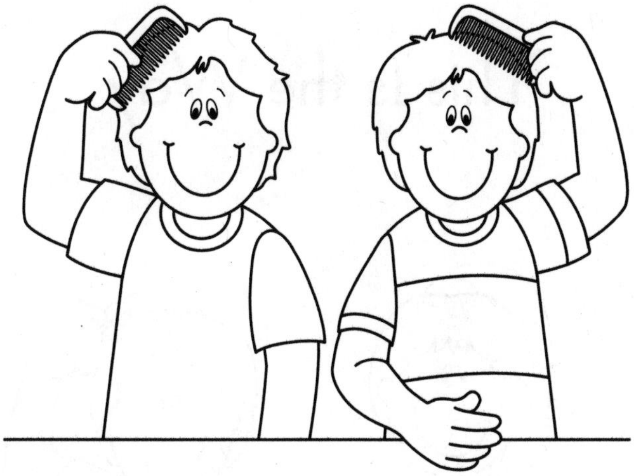

This is the way we
comb our hair,
comb our hair,
comb our hair.

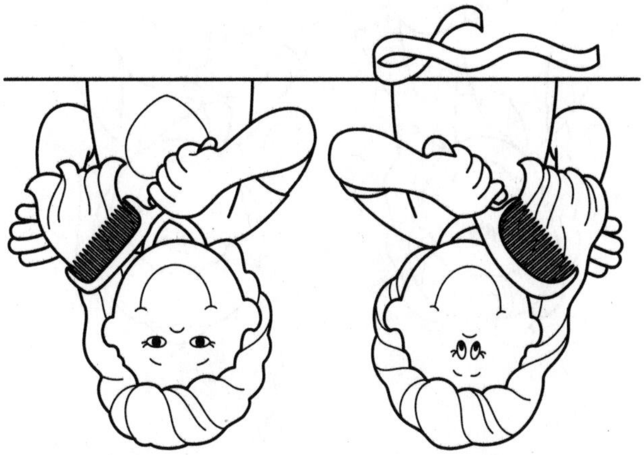

This is the way we
comb our hair,
So early in the morning.

This is the way
we zip our pants,
we zip our pants,
we zip our pants.

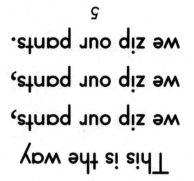

This is the way
we zip our pants,
So early in the morning.

This Is the Way

Illustrated and read by

____

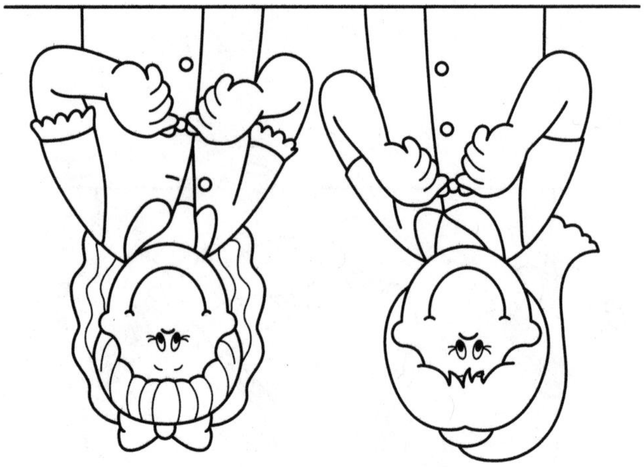

This is the way we
button our shirts,
button our shirts,
button our shirts.

3

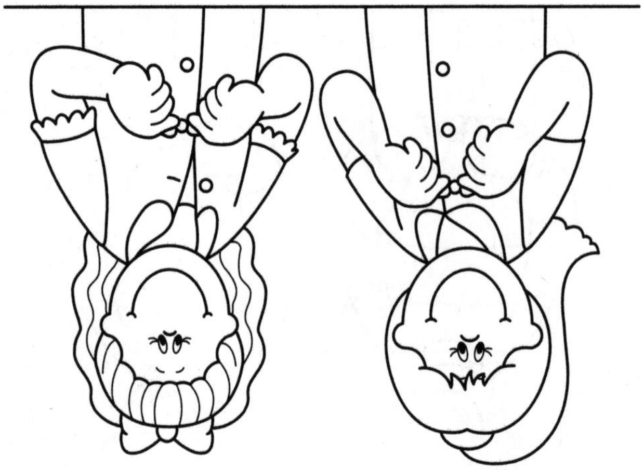

This is the way we
button our shirts,
So early in the morning.

4

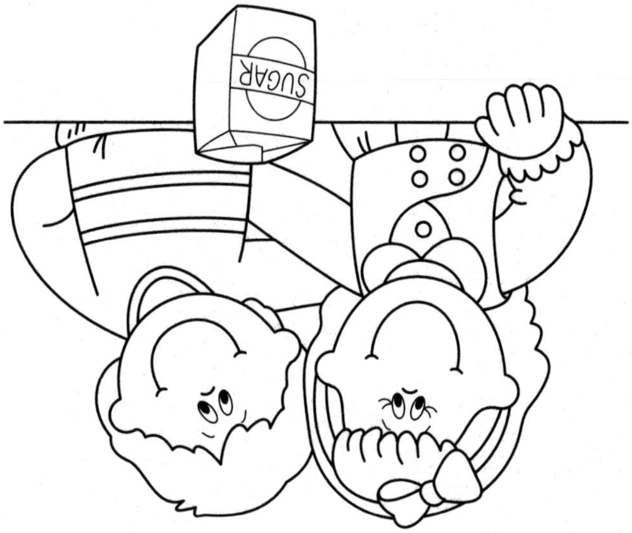

Sugar is sweet,
And so are you.

2

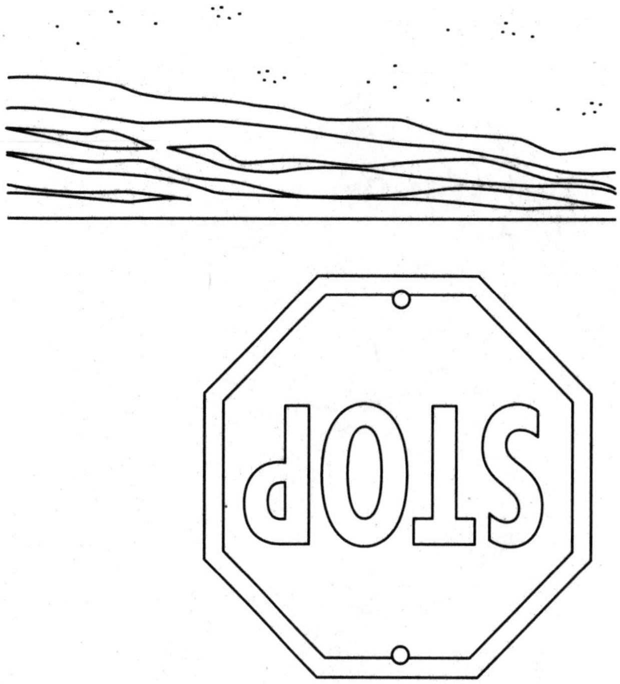

Stop signs are red,
Oceans are blue,

5

Roses are red,
Violets are blue,

1

Candy is sweet,
And so are you.

6

Roses Are Red

Illustrated and read by

____

Hearts are red,
Skies are blue,

3

Honey is sweet,
And so are you.

4

I like ____________________.

__________ is

__________________________.

1

The stories are

__________________________.

2

I like books!

5

Written, illustrated, and read by

____

6

I like ____________.

He is ____________.

3

The stories are ____________.

4

Published by a member of

____

Class

Books

2

My hair is

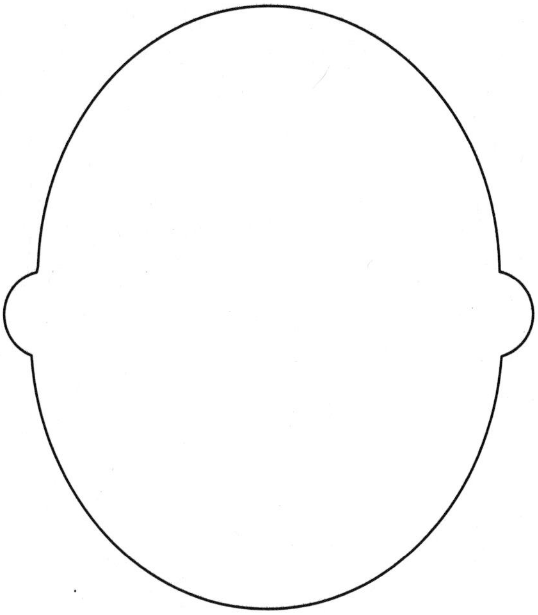

_______________.

5

I am just right!

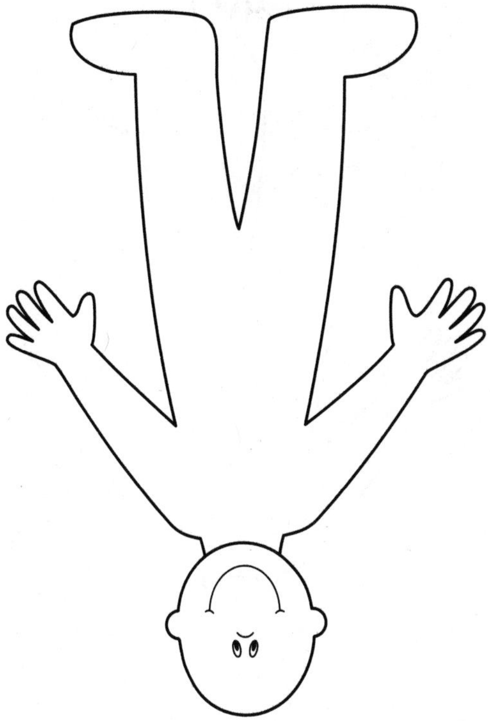

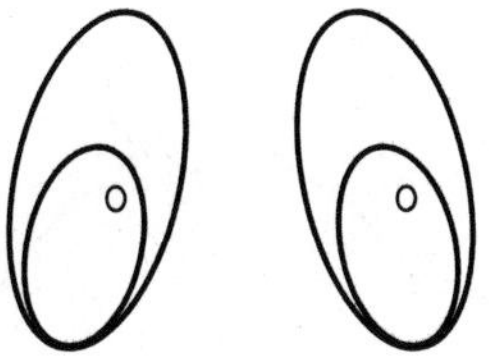

My eyes are

_______________.

1

Written, illustrated, and read by

____

6

Me

Published by a member of

____

Class

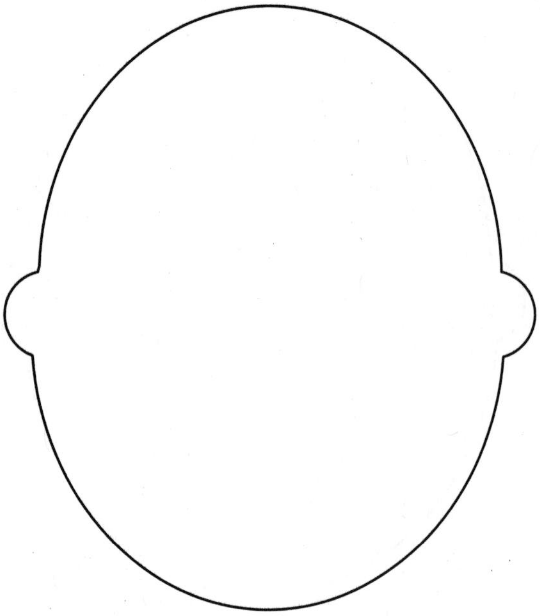

My smile is ____________________.

3

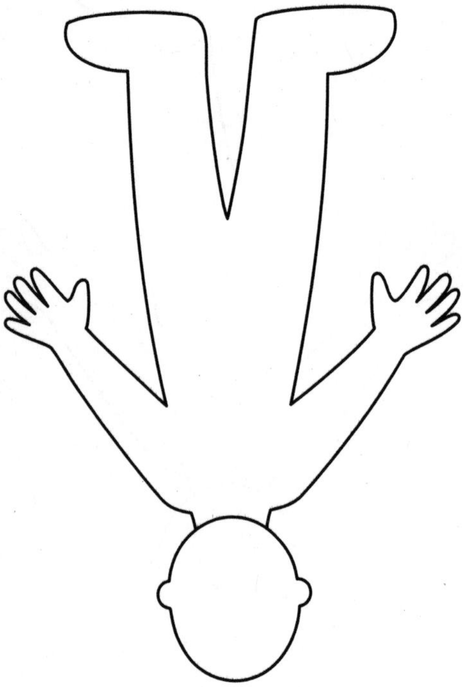

I am ____________________.

4

I have ________ people in my family.

2

We like to ________ together.

5

This is my family.

1

I love my family.

6

My Family

Written, illustrated, and read by

____

I am the ______________.

3

We live in a ______________.

4

I have ________________ friends.

1

We like to ________________.

2

I am glad I have friends.

5

Written, illustrated, and read by

____

6

124

My Friends

Published by a member of

____

Class

We like to

____________________.

3

A good friend

____________________.

4

I have ____________, ____________, and ____________.

2

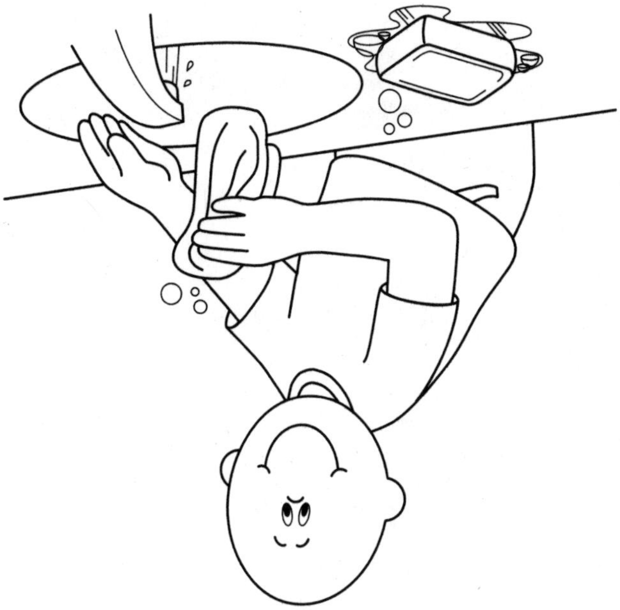

I take good care of my body.

5

My body is very special.

1

Written, illustrated, and read by

____

6

The most useful part of my body ________.

3

I like my ________ because ________.

4

Published by a member of

____

Class

My Body

I wear clothes.

1

I have on a ________

________.

2

My clothes keep my

________.

5

Written, illustrated, and read by

____

6

I have on ______________ ______________.

3

I wear ______________ shoes.

4

Clothing

____

Published by a member of

____

Class

There is a red

________.

1

and a purple

________.

6

There is an orange

________.

2

There is a blue

____

5

There is a green ________.

4

There is a yellow ________.

3

Written, illustrated, and read by

____

There Is a Rainbow in My Classroom

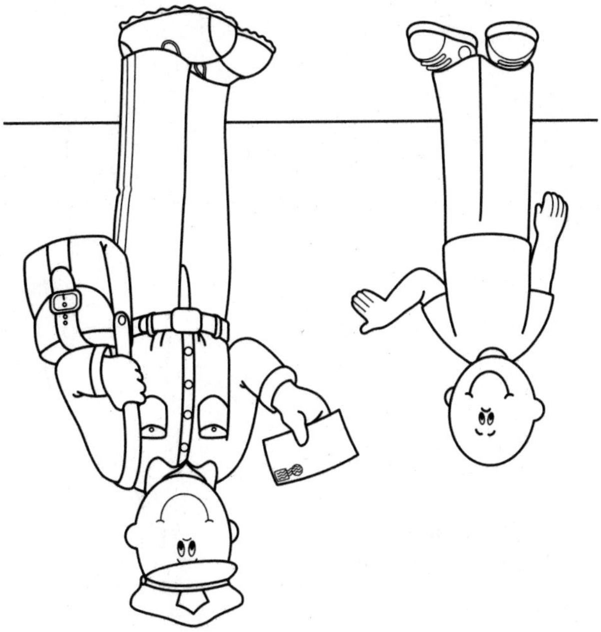

The mail carrier delivers it to your ________.

2

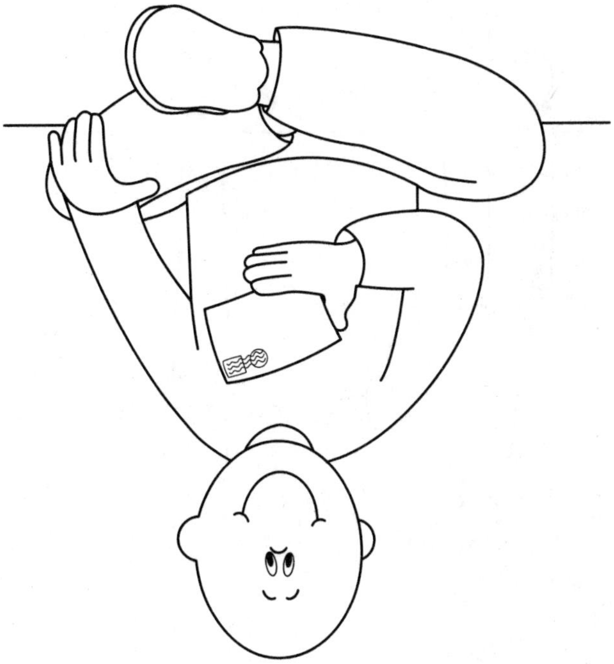

It is fun to get mail!

5

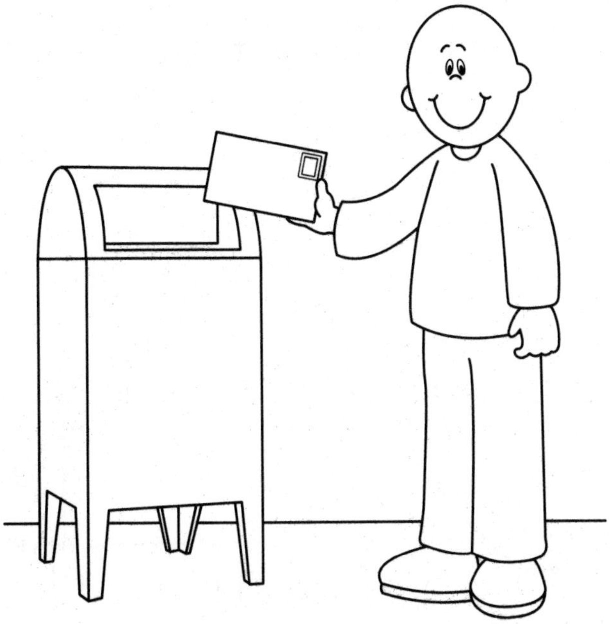

You mail a letter.

1

Written, illustrated, and read by

____

6

Post Office

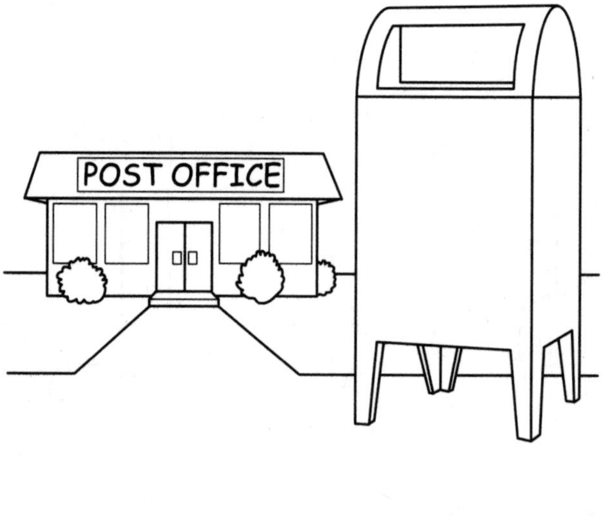

Published by a member of

____

Class

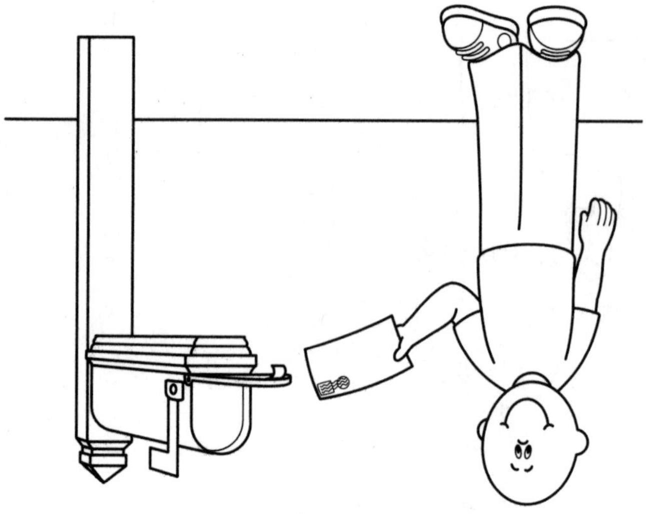

Your __________ is so happy ______ sends ________ a postcard.

3

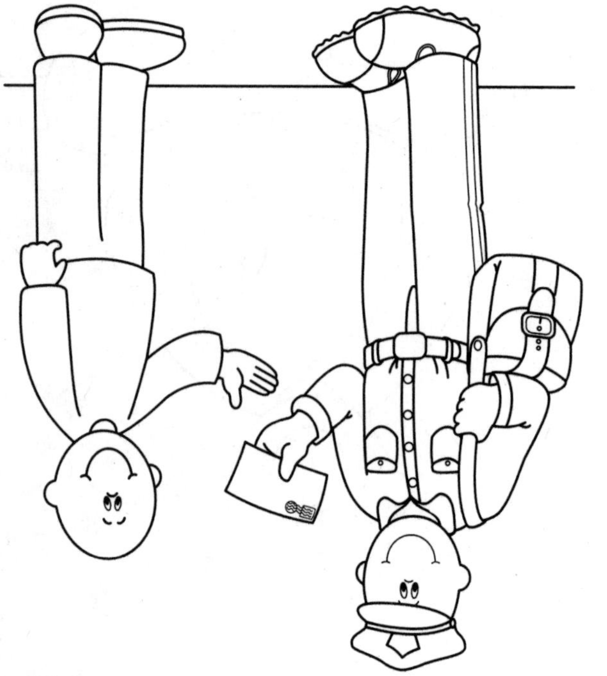

And the mail carrier delivers it to your __________.

4

We will take a

_______________.

2

We think trips are fun!

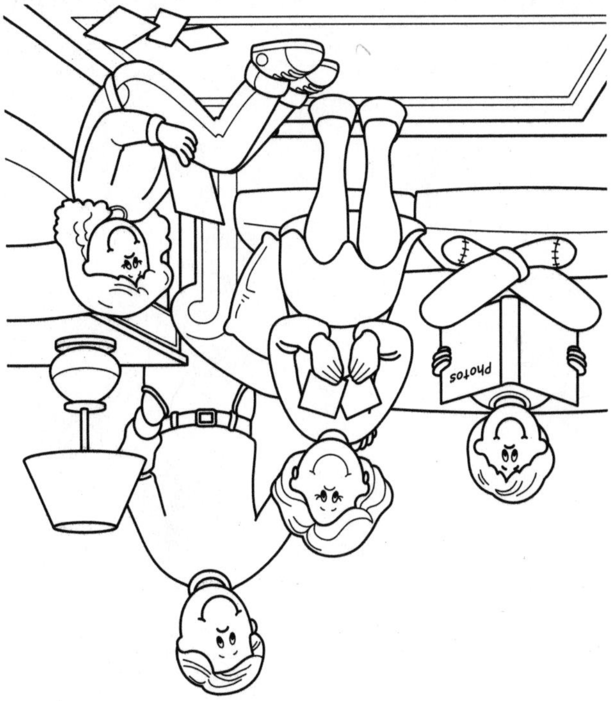

5

We're going on a trip.

1

Written, illustrated, and read by

____

6

3

We will stay ______________.

4

When we get there, we will go ______________.

Travel

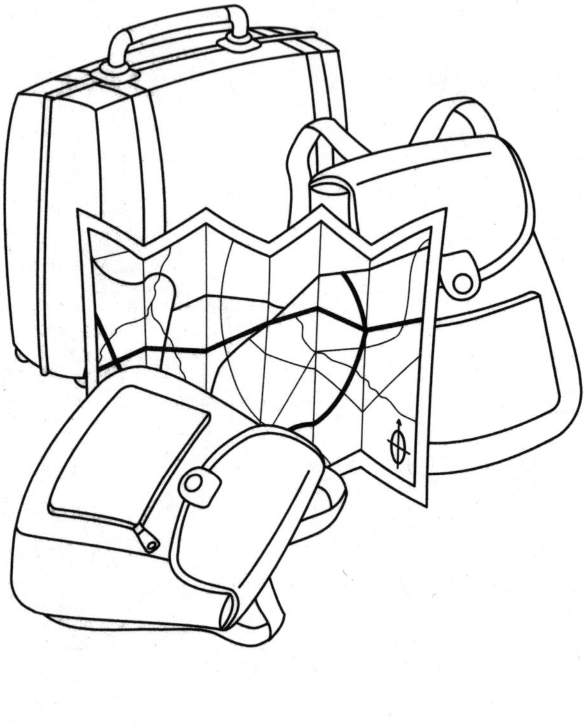

Published by a member of

____

Class

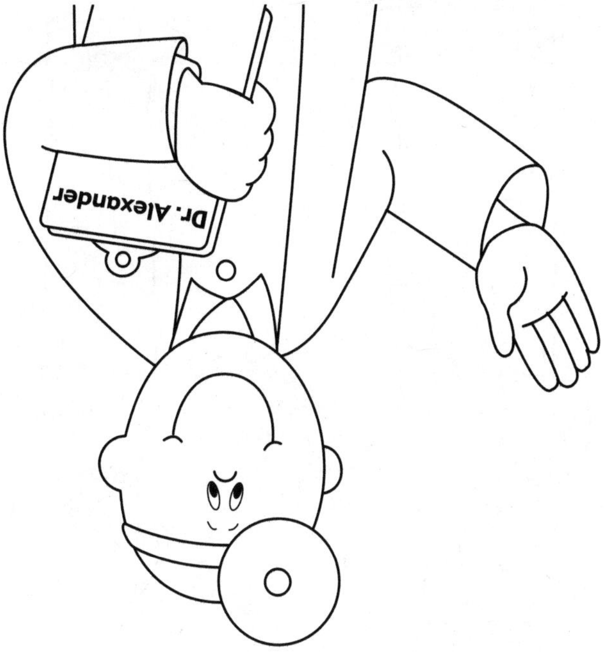

My doctor is ____________.

2

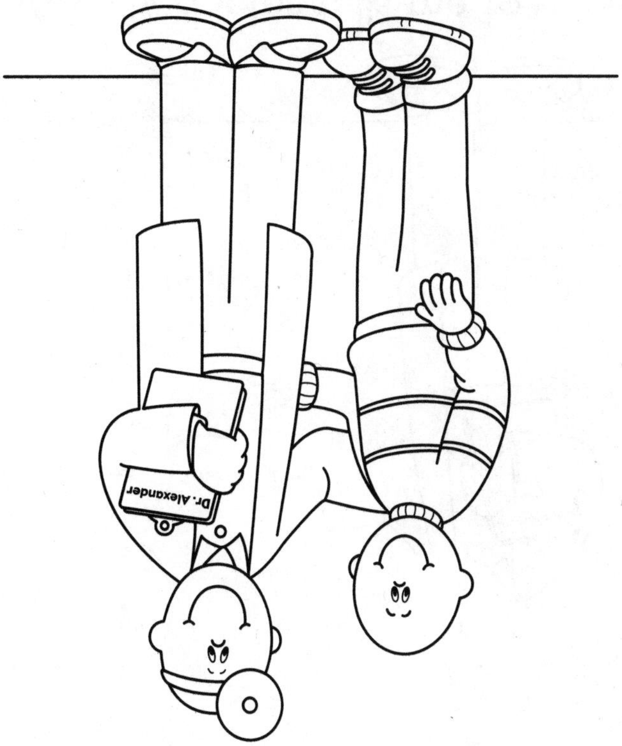

I like my doctor.

5

I go to see the doctor.

1

Written, illustrated, and read by

____

6

Doctor's Office

Published by a member of

____

Class

My doctor gives me

_______________________.

3

My doctor tells me to

_______________________.

4

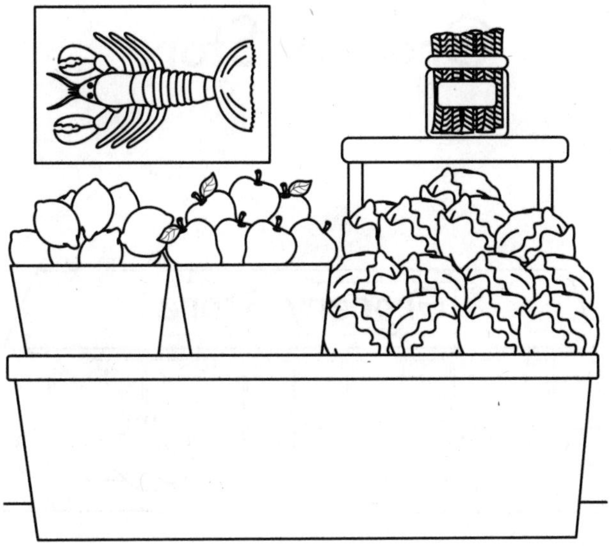

The grocery store is
a neat place.

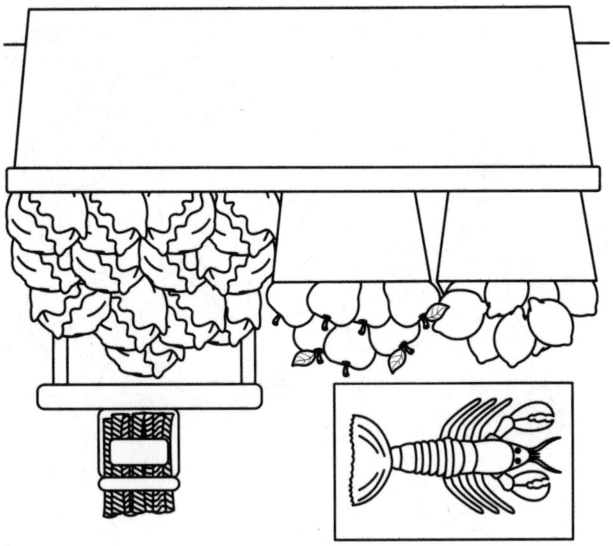

It has

_______________.

The best part of the grocery store is

_______________.

Written, illustrated, and read
by

____

4

When I go, I

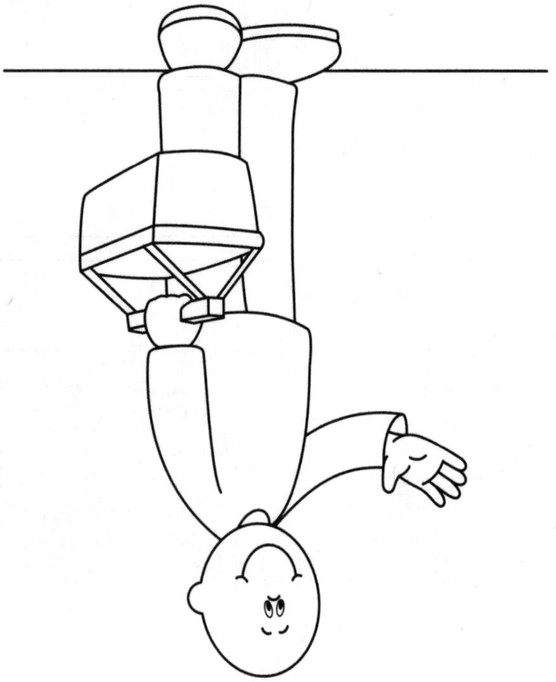

3

It has

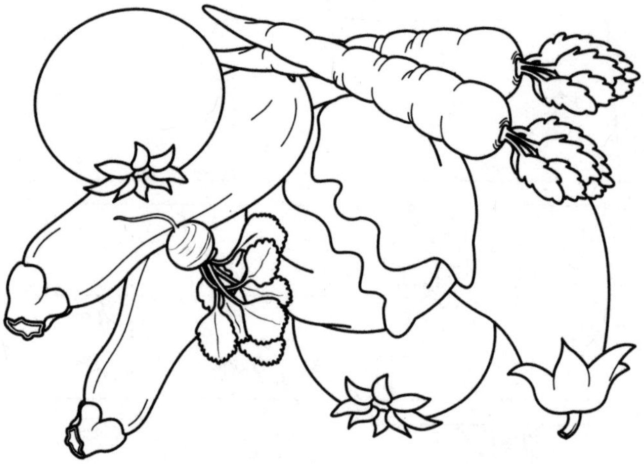

Published by a member of

Class

Grocery Store

2

We go to ________.

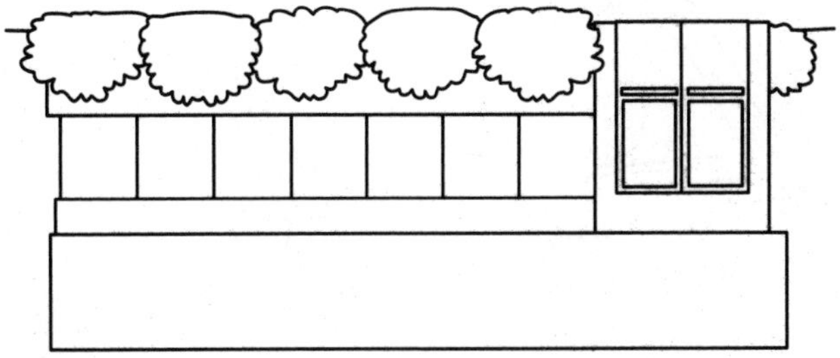

5

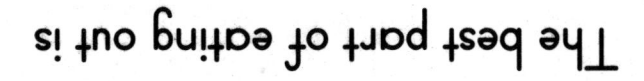

The best part of eating out is ________.

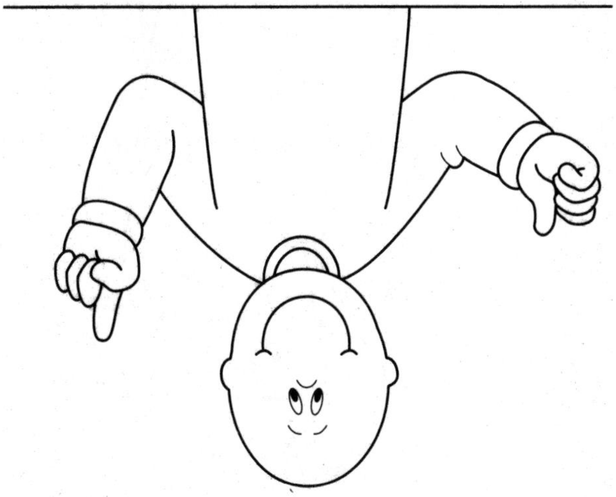

We go out to eat.

1

Written, illustrated, and read by

____

6

4

I drink ____________.

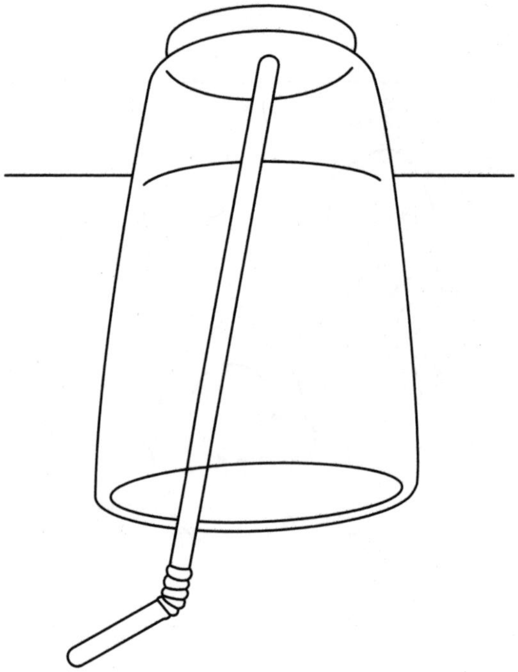

3

We order ____________.

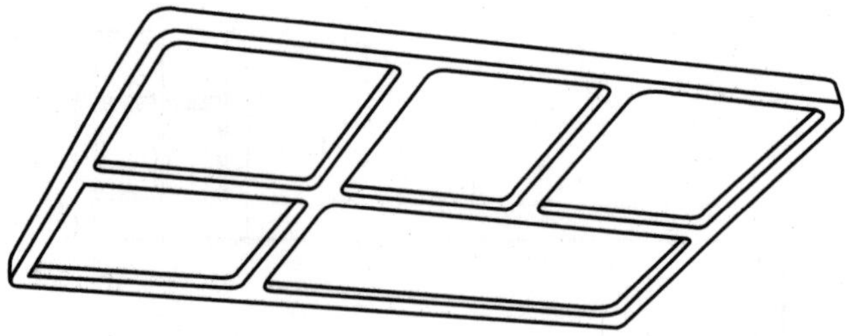

Published by a member of

____

Class

Restaurants

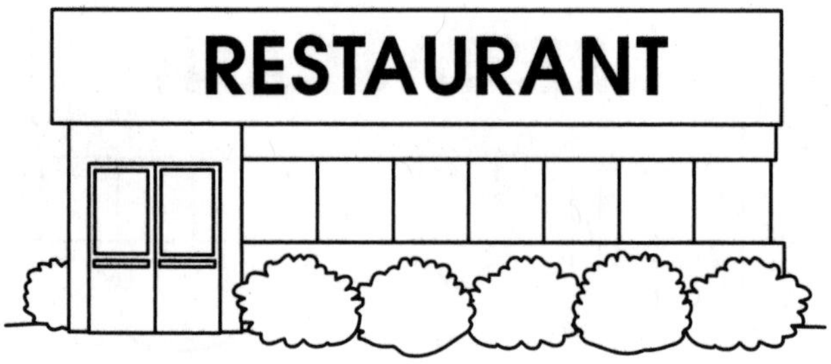

My grandfather and I

______________________________.

1

My grandmother and I

______________________________.

2

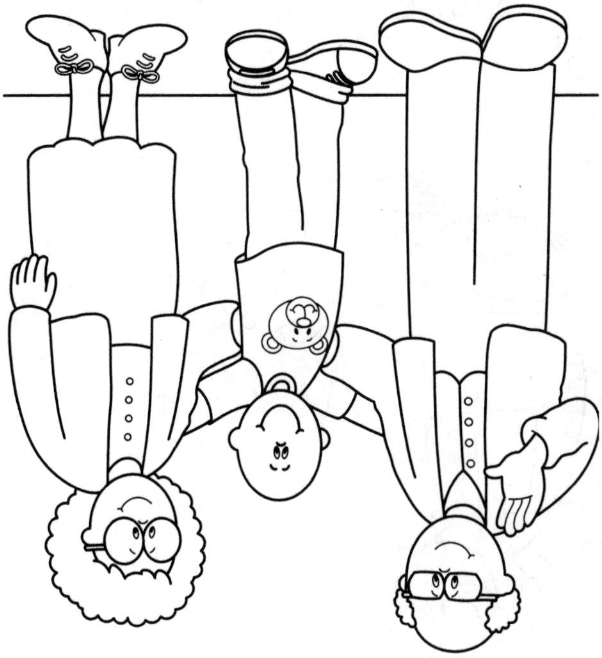

My grandparents are great!

5

Written, illustrated, and read by

____

6

My grandparents and I

3

I see my grandparents

4

Grandparents' Day

Published by a member of

____

Class

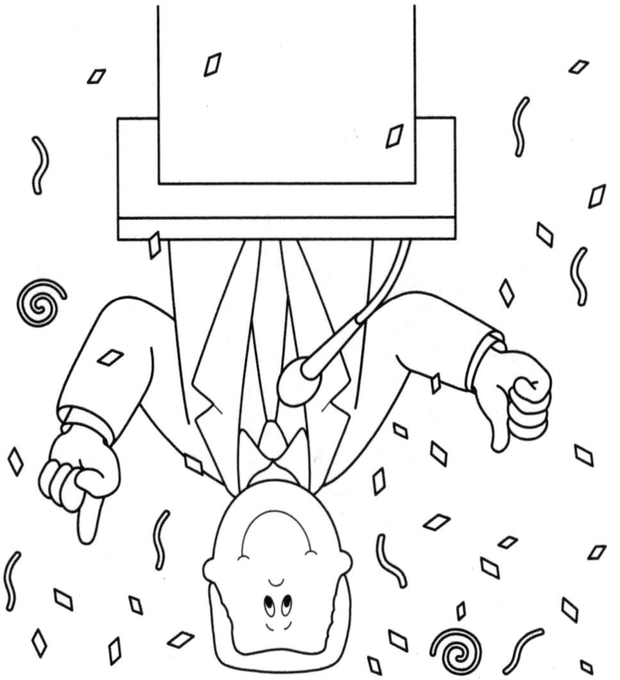

Presidents

2

On Presidents' Day, we remember

5

Presidents' Day is

1

Written, illustrated, and read by

6

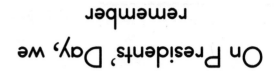

They ______________.

President ______________

is our president.

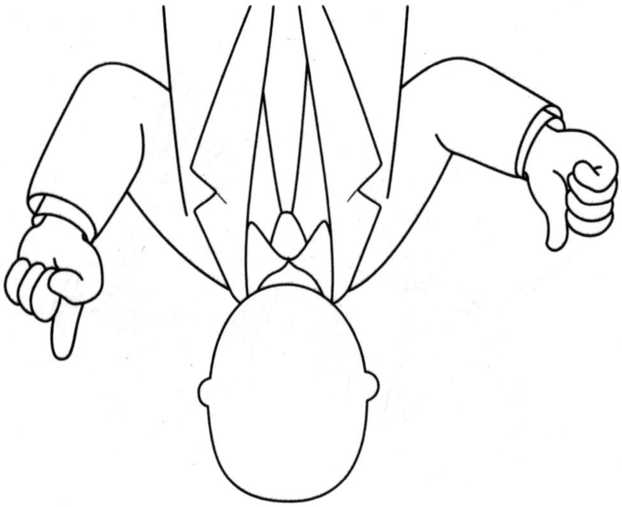

Published by a member of

____

Class

Presidents' Day

I can find

______, ______,

and ______.

2

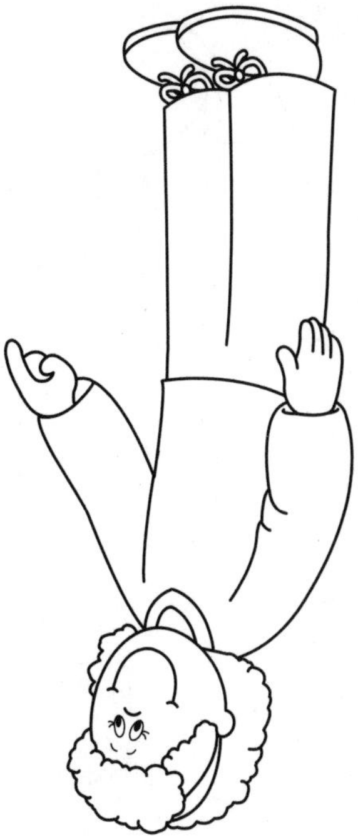

I like the ______ best

because it

______.

5

145

There are bugs on the playground.

1

Written, illustrated, and read by

______

6

The ____________ is the largest.

4

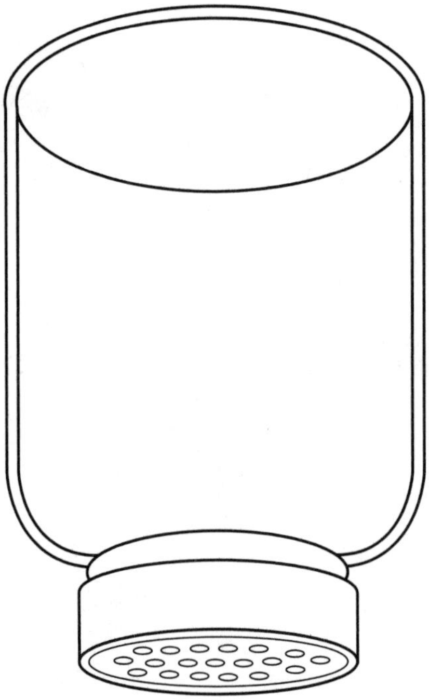

The ____________ is the smallest.

3

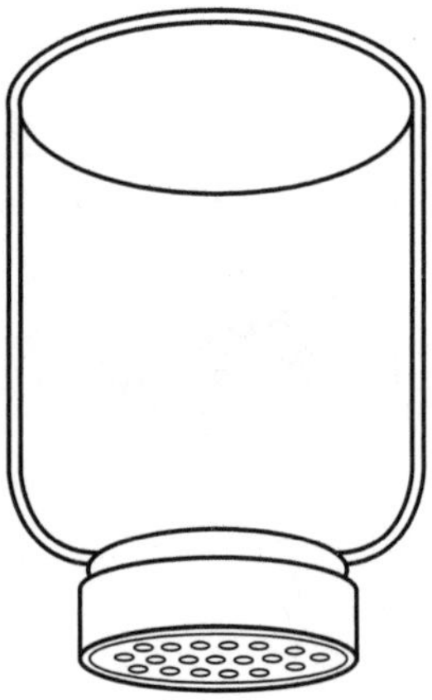

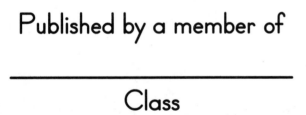

Published by a member of

____

Class

Bugs

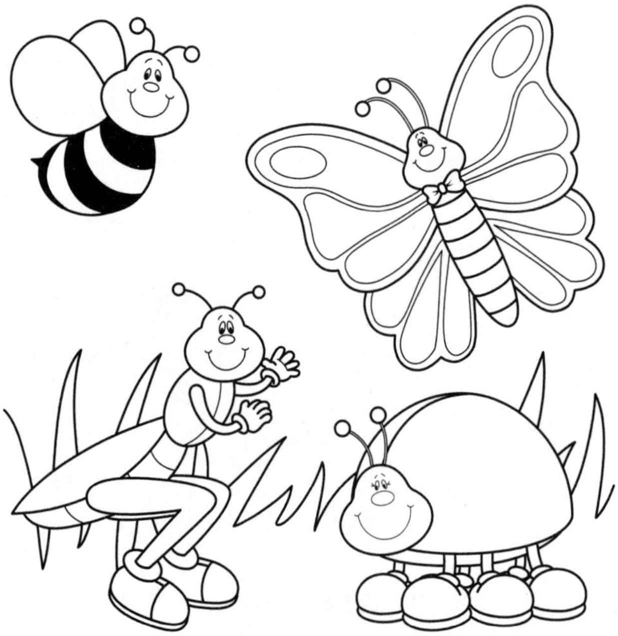

They have ________.

2

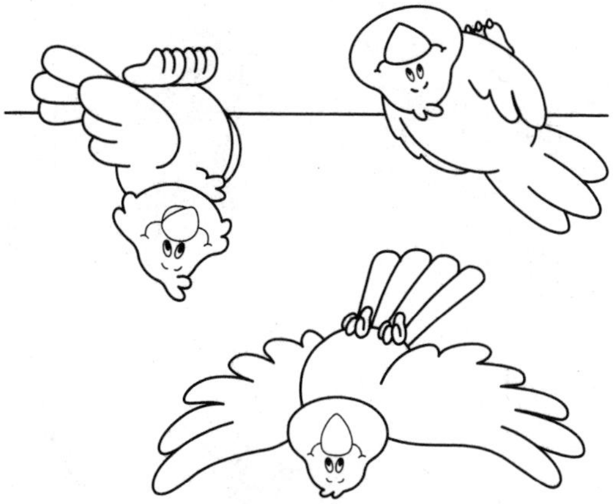

They eat ________.

5

We see birds in the trees.

1

Written, illustrated, and read by

____

6

Some are ____________.

4

They have

____________.

3

Published by a member of

____

Class

Birds

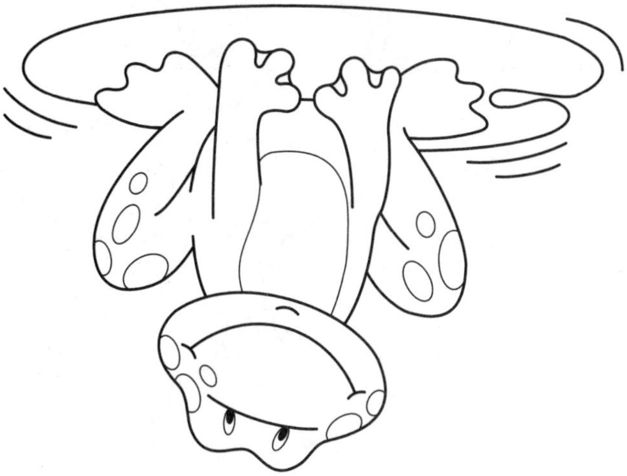

Frogs are

They live

Frogs and toads are

Written, illustrated, and read
by

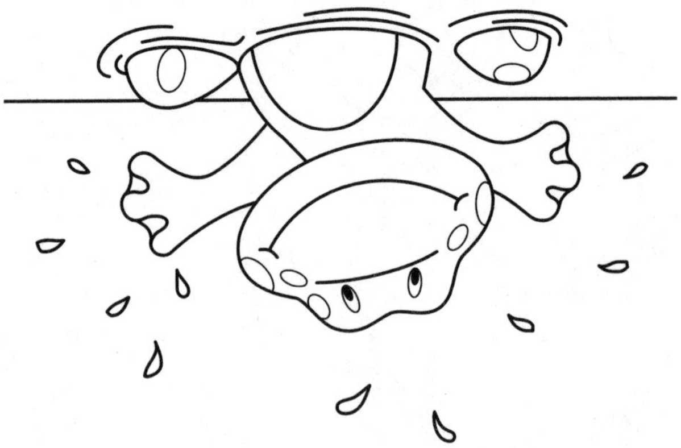

They live

____________________.

3

Toads are

____________________.

4

Frogs and Toads

Published by a member of

____

Class

2

Dogs are pets.

5

They ________.

Pets are great.

1

Fish are pets.

6

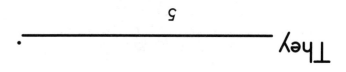

Cats are pets.

They ______________.

They ______________.

Pets

It is winter.

1

In the winter, ______ it.

2

Winter is great because ______.

5

Written, illustrated, and read by

______

6

We make ________.

4

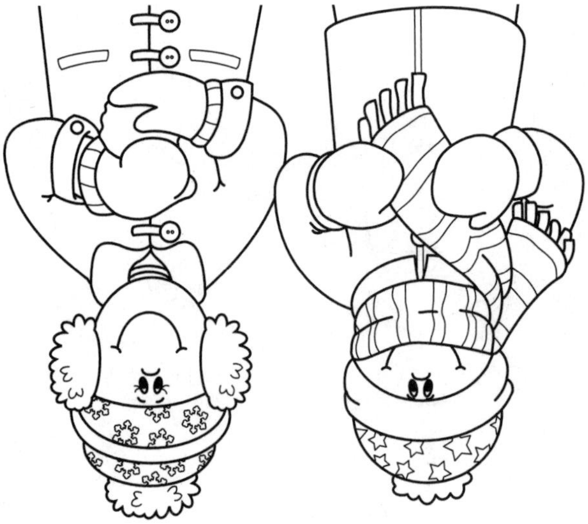

We wear ________.

3

Published by a member of

____

Class

Winter

2

In the spring, ______.

5

Spring is great because the rain makes the flowers grow.

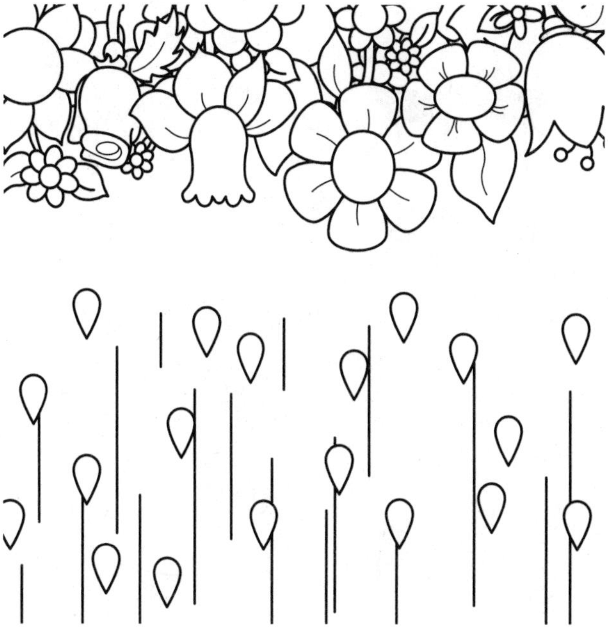

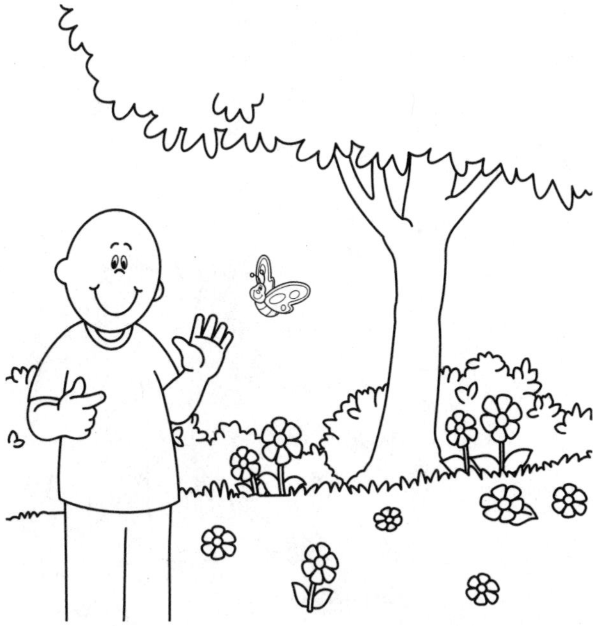

It is spring.

1

Written, illustrated, and read by

______

6

We 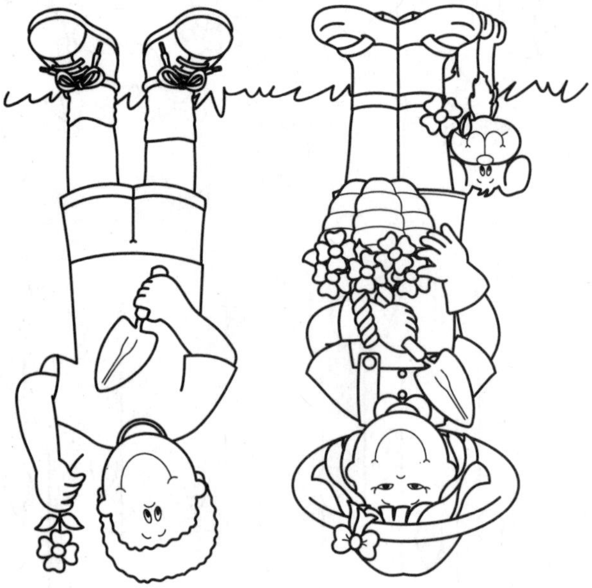

We wear 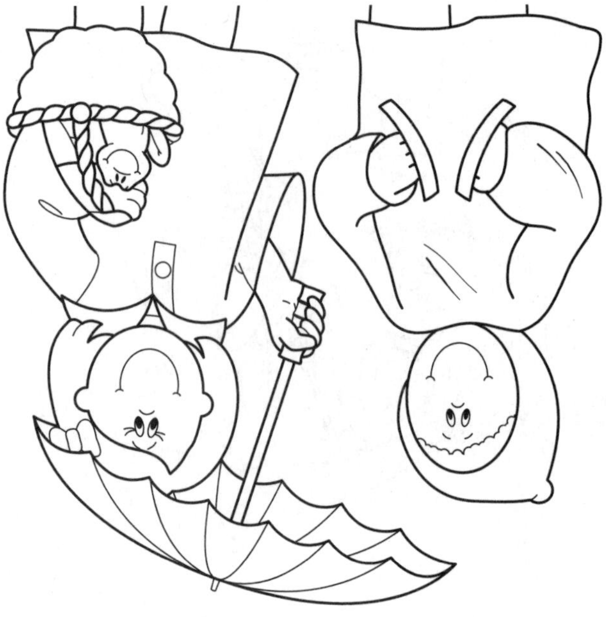

Published by a member of

Class

Spring

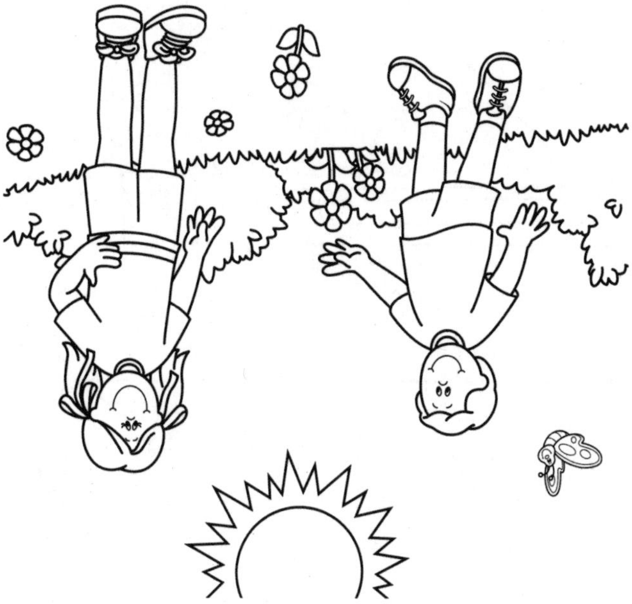

In the summer it is ________________.

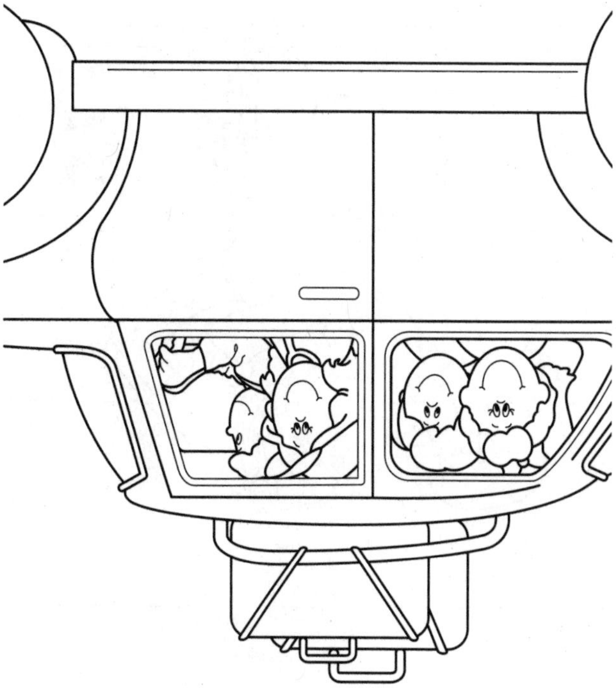

Summer is great because we ________________.

Soon it will be summer.

Written, illustrated, and read
by

____

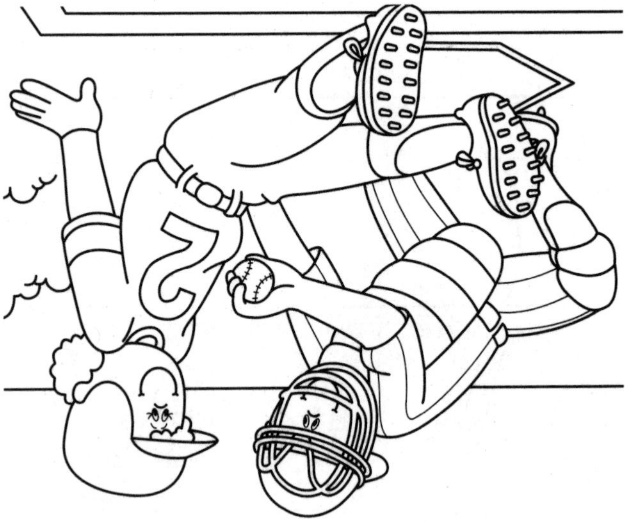

We play ________.

4

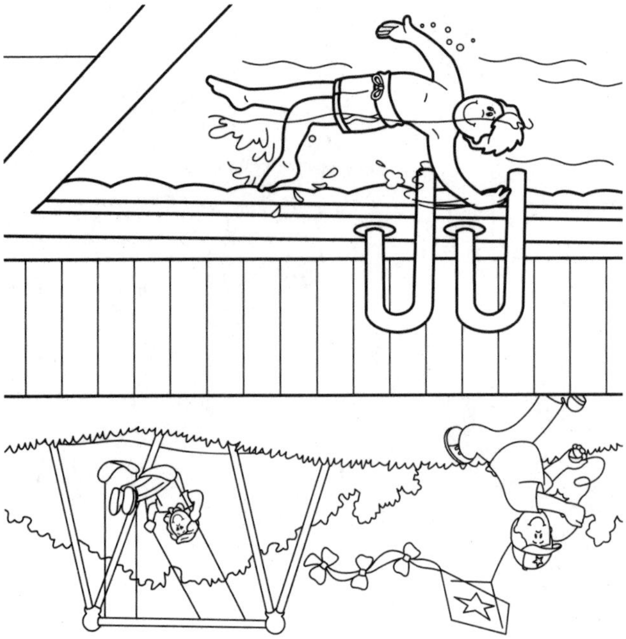

We go ________.

3

Summer

Published by a member of

____

Class

2

In the fall,

5

Fall is great because

After summer comes fall.

1

Written, illustrated, and read
by

6

4

We go

3

The leaves

Published by a member of

Class

Fall

Rocks are ________________.

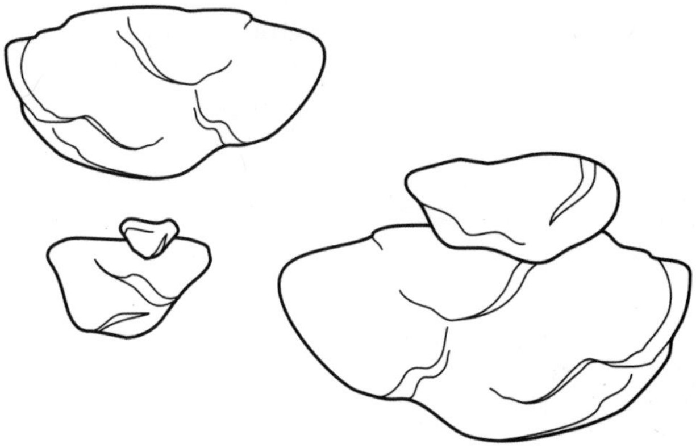

We use rocks to build ________________.

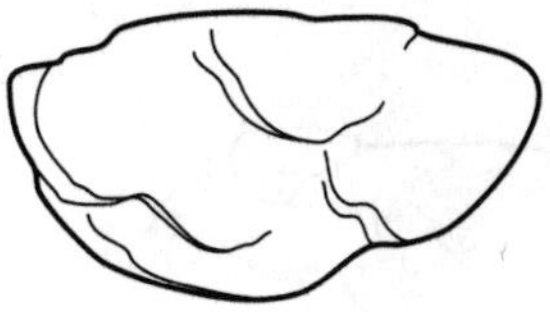

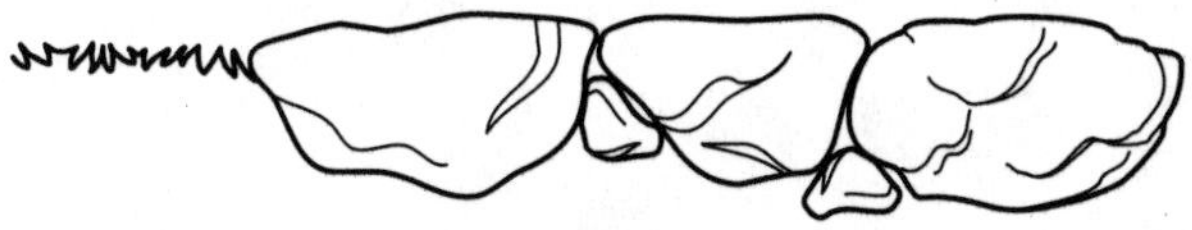

The earth is made of rocks.

Illustrated and read

by

____

Rocks can be

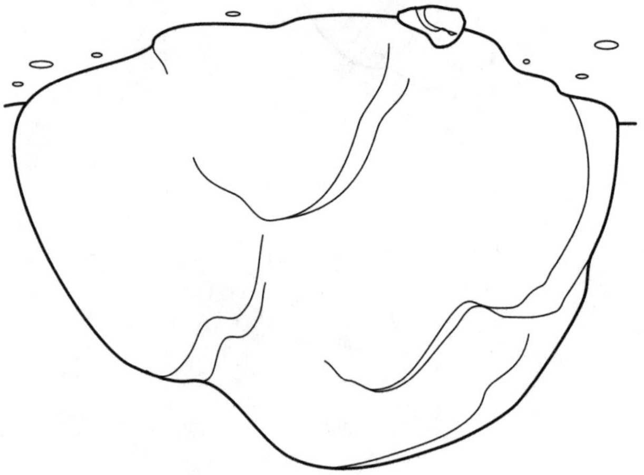

______________________.

4

Rocks can be

______________________.

3

Published by a member of

____

Class

Rocks

The sun ________.

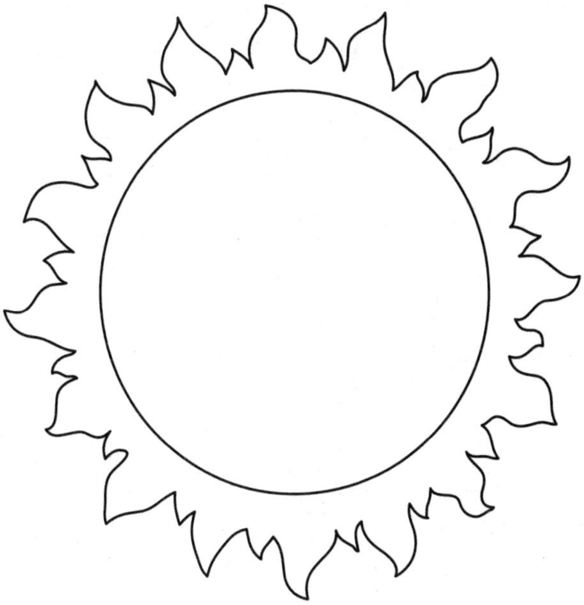

It ________.

The sun and moon
are in the sky.

Written, illustrated, and read
by

____

The moon ________.

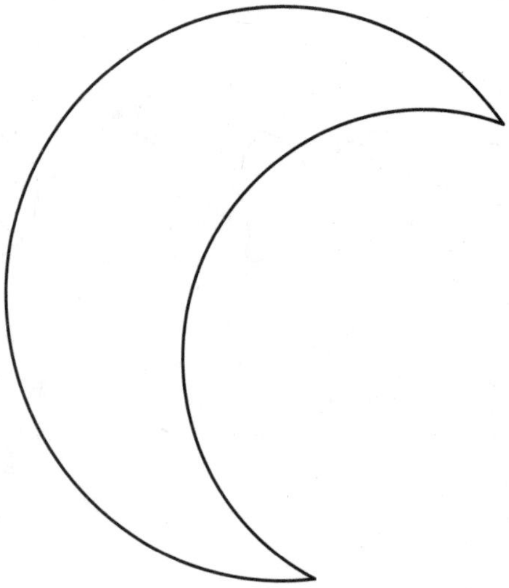

It ________.

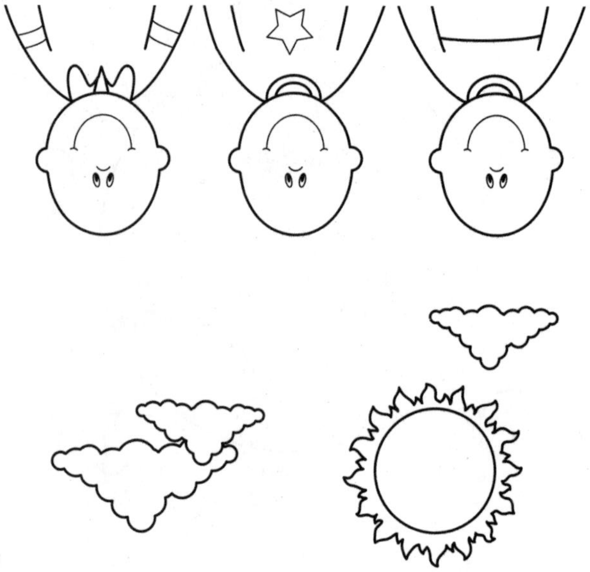

Published by a member of

____

Class

Sun and Moon

Sometimes it is

____________________.

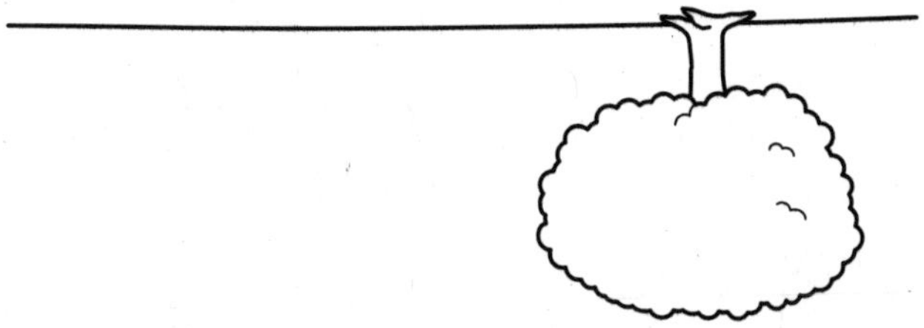

2

We get air to breathe from the sky.

5

The sky is all around us.

1

Written, illustrated, and read by

____

6

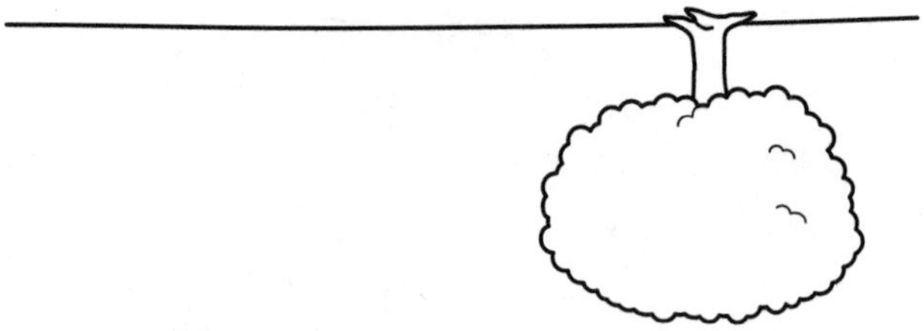

fly ________ through the sky.

4

falls ________ from the sky.

3

Published by a member of

____

Class

The Sky

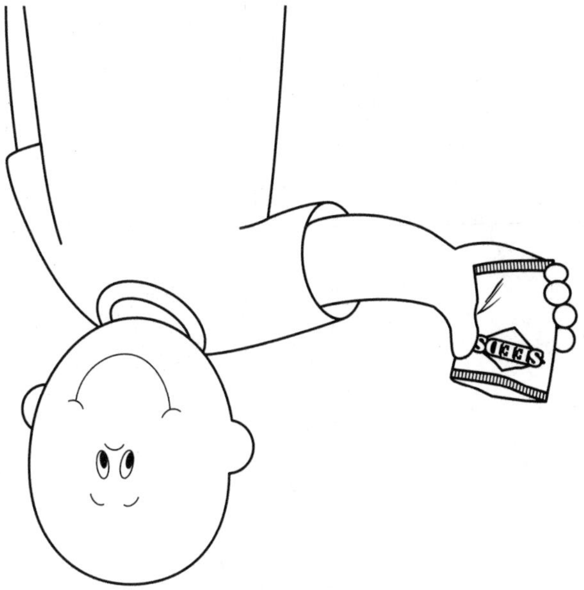

I will plant

_____________.

2

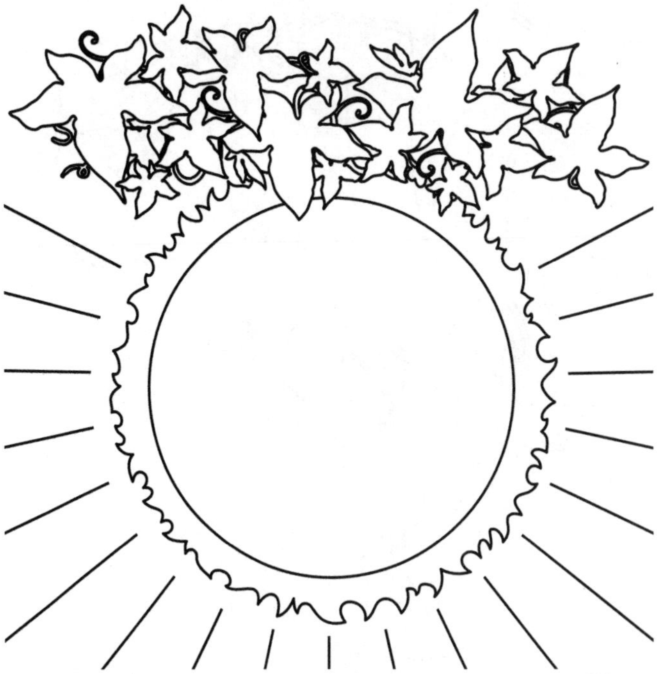

Plants need

_____________.

5

We see plants on our earth.

1

Written, illustrated, and read by

____

6

Plants

Published by a member of

____

Class

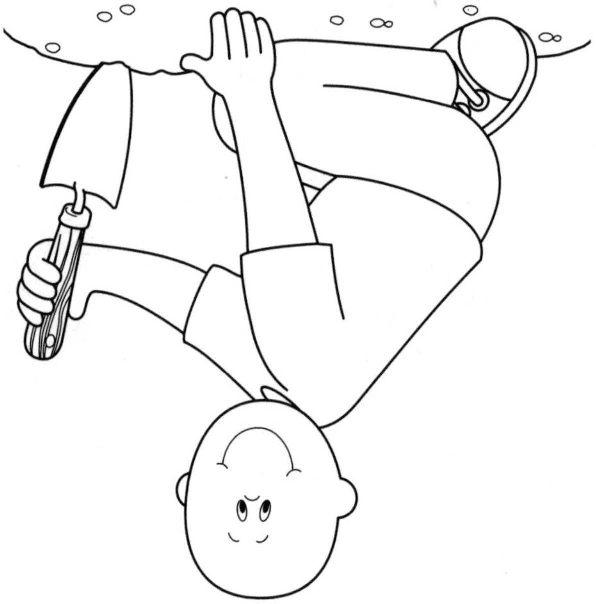

I will need

____________________.

3

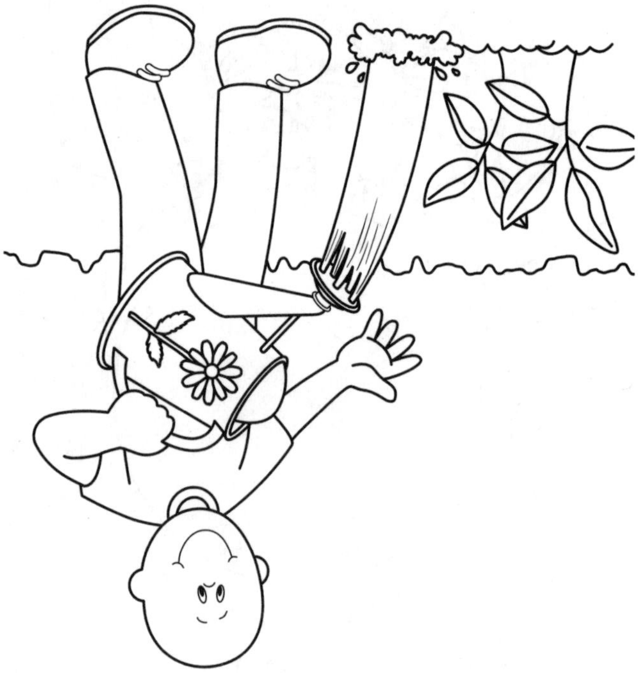

Plants need

____________________.

4

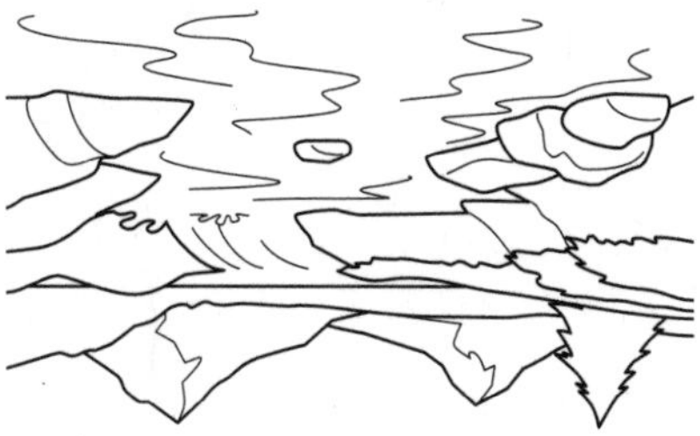

Water can be found in ______.

2

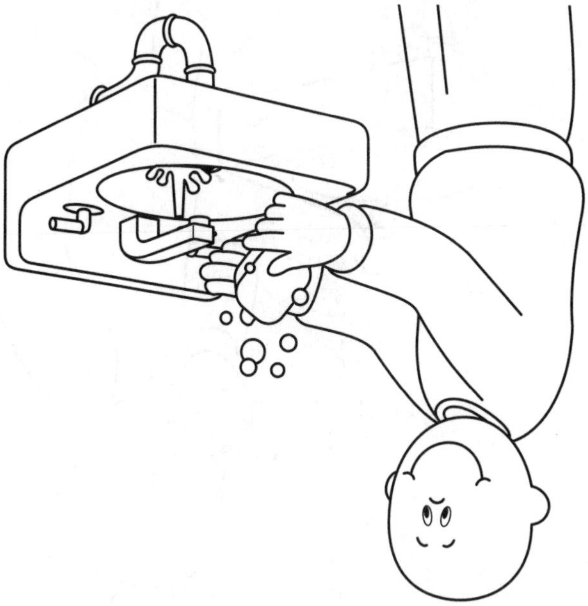

We use water to ______.

5

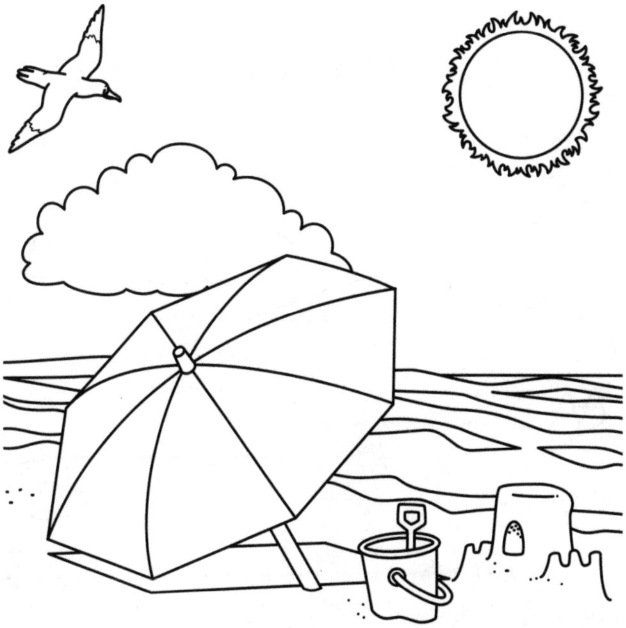

Our earth is made
of lots of water.

1

We need to take care of
the water on our earth.

6

4

We use water to

______.

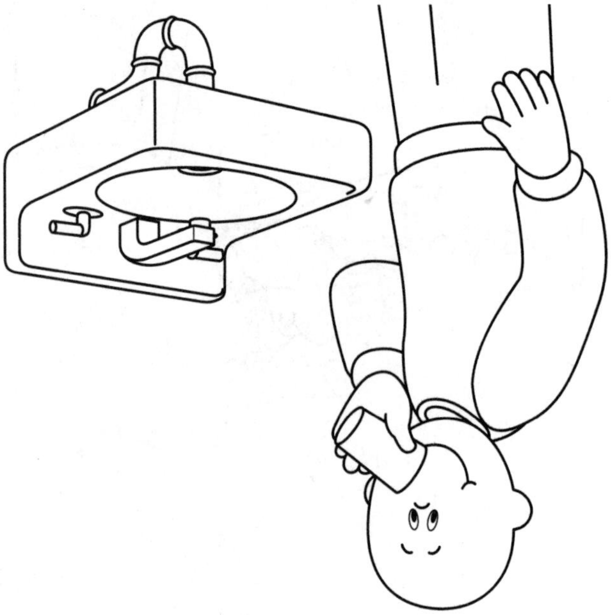

3

______ need water.

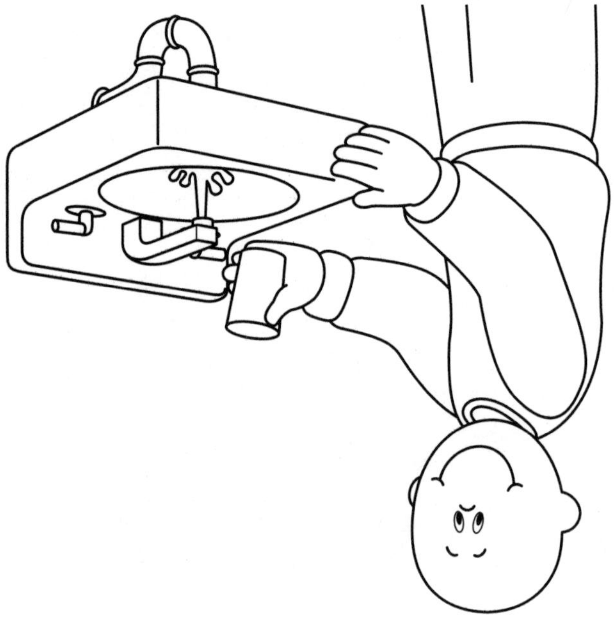

Written, illustrated, and read by

______

Water

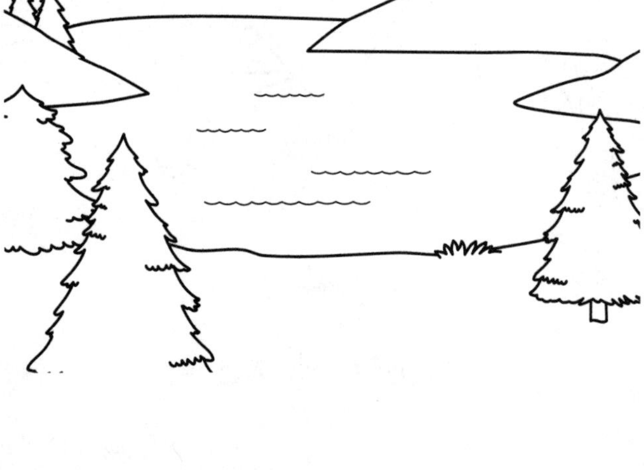

Machines do work.

1

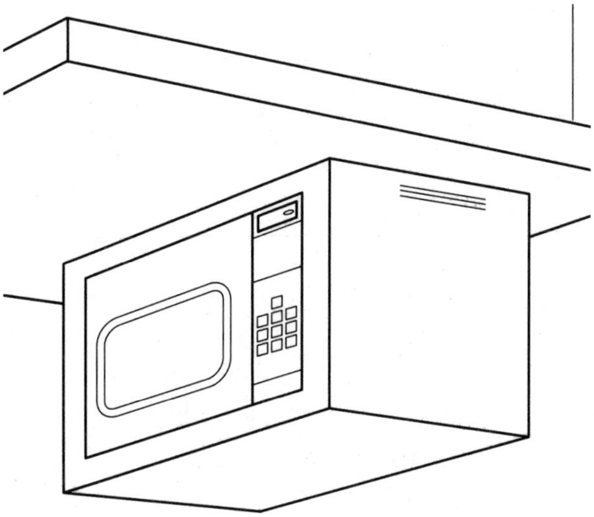

A ____________ is a machine.

2

A ____________ is another machine.

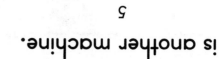

5

Written, illustrated, and read by

____

6

4

It is ________.

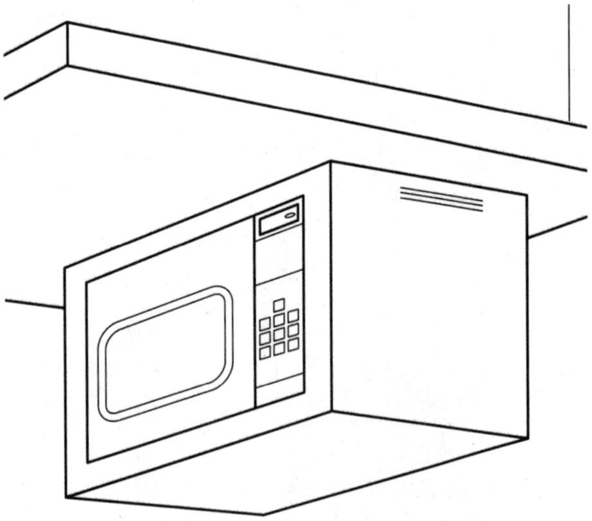

3

It helps us ________.

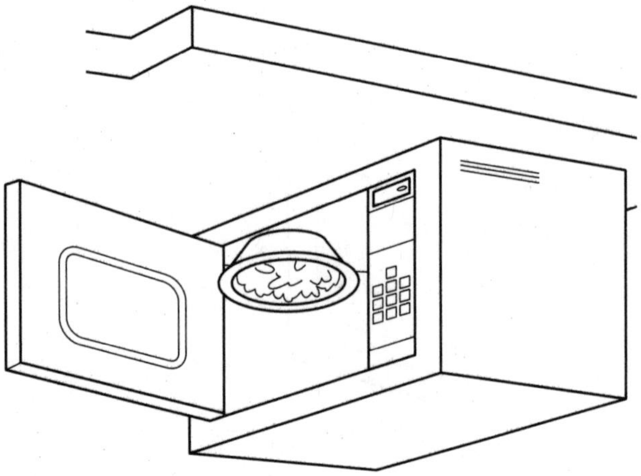

Published by a member of

____

Class

Machines

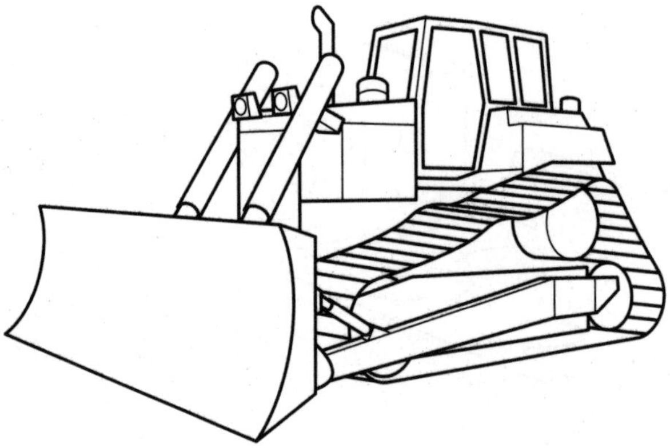

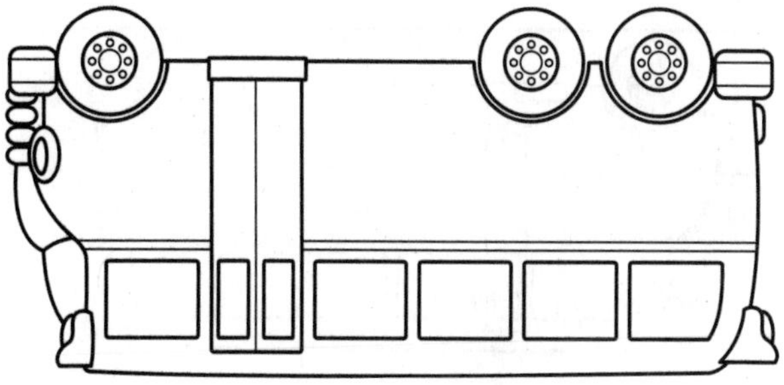

A bus is transportation.

2

I would like to take a trip on a ______________.

13

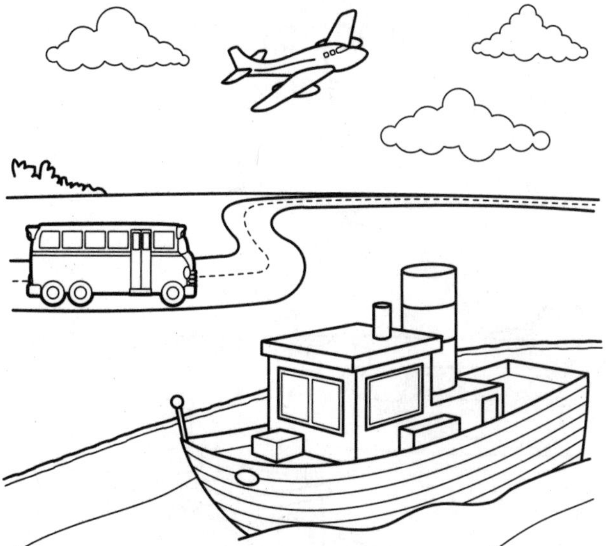

Transportation takes people and things places.

1

Written, illustrated, and read by

____

14

My favorite transportation is ______.

12

It travels on roads.

3

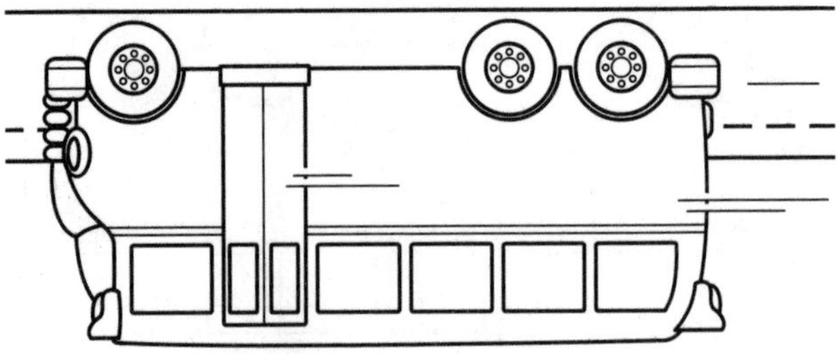

Published by a member of

______

Class

Transportation

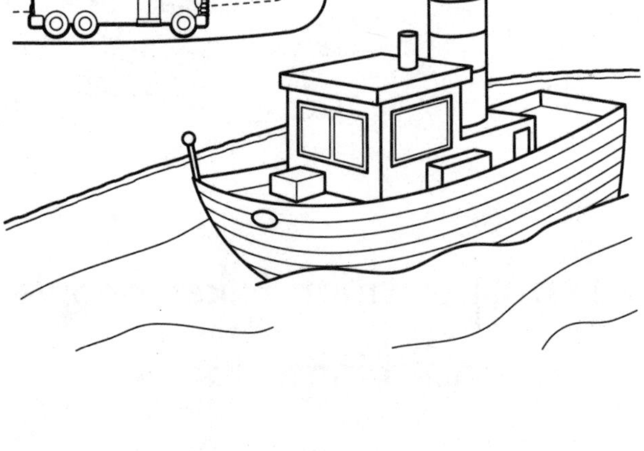

6

It travels on water.

9

It travels in the air.

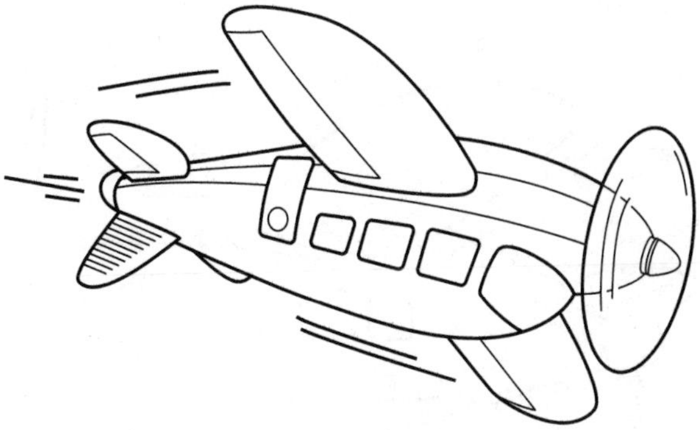

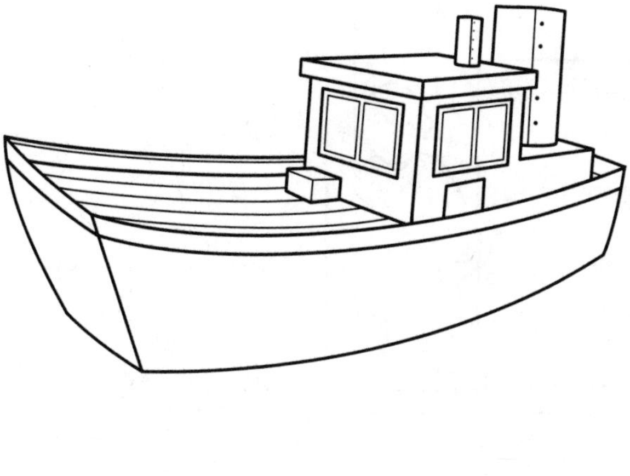

A boat is transportation.

5

It carries mail.

10

A plane is transportation.

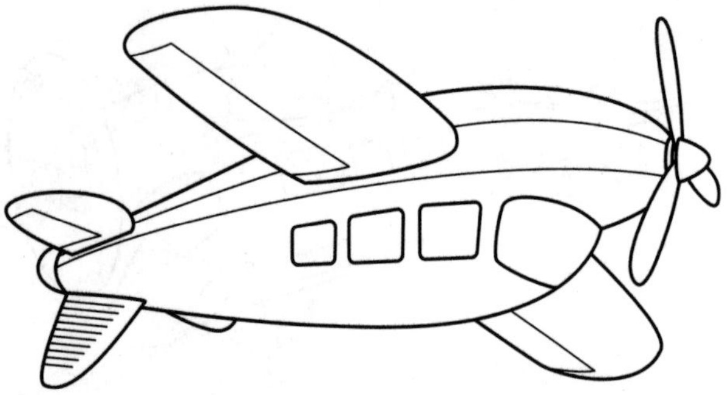

8

It carries boxes.

7

I have taken a trip on a

_____________________________.

11

It carries people.

4